NOTES OF A NATIVE DAUGHTER

THEOLOGICAL EDUCATION BETWEEN THE TIMES

Ted A. Smith, series editor

Theological Education between the Times gathers diverse groups of people for critical, theological conversations about the meanings and purposes of theological education in a time of deep change. The project is funded by the Lilly Endowment Inc.

NOTES OF
A NATIVE DAUGHTER

Testifying in Theological Education

Keri Day

WILLIAM B. EERDMANS PUBLISHING COMPANY

GRAND RAPIDS, MICHIGAN

Wm. B. Eerdmans Publishing Co.
4035 Park East Court SE, Grand Rapids, Michigan 49546
www.eerdmans.com

Published 2021
Printed in the United States of America

27 26 25 24 23 22 21   1 2 3 4 5 6 7

ISBN 978-0-8028-7882-3

Library of Congress Cataloging-in-Publication Data

A catalog record for this book is available from the Library
    of Congress.

Contents

Acknowledgments

I am grateful that I have been able to see this manuscript through to completion. It has been a joy to write it and to have so many people along the way who encouraged and assisted me during this project. I first want to thank Ted Smith, who invited me to be one of twelve scholars who would write small books on transformations in theological education. I must admit that when he first approached me, I was apprehensive about participating. In part, I wasn't sure if I had anything to *say* that had not already been written by scholars of color about the current state and potential futures of theological education. After thinking about this opportunity, I realized that what was needed wasn't so much saying something new as saying something truthful and authentic about what black scholars such as myself experience within the theological academy. This book not only has allowed me to look back to the "great cloud of witnesses" that formed my early childhood, it has also empowered me to dream about "otherwise" futures within theological education, that is, futures *other than* those usually considered. Ted, thanks for this invitation. Writing this book has changed my life.

I also want to acknowledge the twelve scholars with whom I wrote, laughed, cried, prayed, and ate for three years in multiple locations around the nation. We were not just a writers' colony; we became family. With each other, we witnessed health renewed, grandchildren born, new marriages, the expansion of families, retirements, new academic posts, and more. We lived through the highs and lows of each other's lives. And we wrote our books out of this rich intimacy and a sense that we belong to each other. I pray that all scholars can experience this kind of community as they fulfill their vocation within theological education. Thank you to this group, as it has shaped me into a more open, caring, and compassionate human being and academic.

To the best editor one could ask for, Ulrike Guthrie: I have grown as a writer in part because of you. Thanks, my friend.

Finally, I want to acknowledge the encouragement that my spouse, Austin Moore, continues to give me. I was able to finish this book in the second trimester of a very difficult pregnancy because of your constant support. You give me good love. Thanks be to God.

Introduction

This small book is about how to bear witness to more liberating futures in theological education. Yet before we can envision potential futures, we must be honest about experiences of trauma, pain, and brokenness that now mark the theological academy. Here I offer extended "notes" or meditations on the struggles so many African Americans confront and endure within theological institutions. My account might be read less as a philosophical argument and more as a *testimony*, a form of speech that unapologetically bears witness to how theological education is experienced among those from the underside of American society.

Testifying is a familiar mode of religious speech for me. I grew up in a black Pentecostal church, and at the center of our worship experience was testimony service. Testimony service was visceral and verbal, emotional and demonstrative, a collective and highly democratic enterprise. Often testimony service ended up being the *entire* worship experience. When one stood up to testify, one offered a narrative of how one had overcome through the work of the Spirit. A woman might stand up and testify, only to hear others respond with cries, laughter, celebration, or even a song. Testifying was a highly unpredictable style of worship, as the Spirit could be felt at any moment, pulling the entire congregation into a series of communal shouts and dances. Most important, testifying was a way to mediate divine presence. When one testified in the midst of the congregation, God's presence was invoked, leading the entire community into experiences of transcendence, deliverance, joy, healing, and so much more. Testifying was not merely an individual act. One didn't tell a story solely for some kind of personal cathartic release or relief. This oral practice formed the community in love, intimacy, and belonging. Even children would lead in testimony service, instructing the adults to testify "as the Spirit gave utterance." Testifying was a communal act; it forged a truly democratic community drawn together by filial bonds of love, care, and accountability. We trusted that God would speak through our sisters and brothers as they testified to God's goodness, mercy, and grace. We uttered our stories in hopes that we would experience the power of the Spirit to be healed and made whole.

This process was not for the faint of heart. Testifying about our stories of God's care involved telling the truth. We told the truth about hard matters. I remember people standing to testify about the social and economic predicaments they faced, telling the truth about the inequality of social structures and economic institutions. Others in the congregation would talk back, nodding their heads or offering high-pitched shouts to affirm that God would deliver the speaker (and themselves) from the hardships of life. I also recall members who would stand and tell hard truths about the congregation—about fights, slights, and bickering among members—in hopes of illuminating the reality of broken community. Sometimes apologies were spoken in testimony service and people would find their way to the person who was wronged, only for screams and shouts to break out in celebration of restored relationships and healing from wounds. Testifying was about bearing witness to a God who could heal in the midst of brokenness and help us face the truth of who we were and could be, if only we could participate in the loving work of the Spirit.

Likewise, in these pages I tell the truth about difficult experiences that mark theological education, not out of spite or bitterness but to demonstrate the toll that broken community takes on all of us. I not only reveal failings of theological and church contexts but also reveal my own shortcomings as I have searched for firmer grounding within these spaces. If we are to be made whole, we must speak the truth as we have experienced it, being transparent about our collective pain even as we await the Spirit's resurrecting power.

Testifying was also prophecy. People would stand up and speak what God revealed to them about the community in terms of its present and future. The testifier reminded us not only to wait on the Spirit but also to work toward the building of beloved communities. This involved vulnerability and openness. We had to be open to what we were getting wrong and repent. Repentance was not simply a verbal apology. It was *metanoia*, conversion. One turned from one's ways when one's actions broke covenant with community.

In this book, I call theological education to repentance by being truthful about the racist character of the theological enterprise even in the midst of its growing racially diverse landscape. Frank Yamada, executive director of the Association of Theological Schools (ATS), notes that the number of black, Latinx, Asian, and Asian North American students in its schools has increased dramatically. By 2040, there will be no majority white (or any) population but a diversity of different sizable populations in the United States. This demographic shift is already becoming a reality for ATS schools. The average seminary student is no longer a young white or European male who is a full-time, residential student. Student populations at ATS schools are increasingly diverse, as students of color "have increased collectively from 30 to 45 percent of the total of ATS students over the past twenty years." Moreover, 20 percent of ATS schools already have a majority of racial ethnic presence in student populations. Yet this increased racial diversity doesn't mean that structural racism has ended. It has merely morphed into new, more subtle forms. For instance, faculty diversity has grown, but at a much slower pace than student diversity, which means that structural racism does not cease to exist simply because of growing diversity, a major point to which I return in chapter 2.[1] Theological schools must wrestle continually with the emotional carnage left in the wake of institutional racial disenfranchisement.

This changing racial/ethnic landscape means that the experiences of marginalized ethnic groups are not peripheral to the present and future of theological education but are central to such conversations. These groups continue to experience real racial harm and trauma. Yet people of color (such as black faculty and students) also are creating and fashioning new theological discourses and practices within the academy itself. This is the tension: the theological academy is a site of both harm and hope for such groups. I give voice to these contradictory realities that often go unacknowledged by institutions that are led and funded by professional white America.

I testify to how I, a native daughter, an African American and Pentecostal scholar, have experienced theological education. I invoke James Baldwin's *Notes of a Native Son* in order to remind the reader that African Americans often experience themselves as native sons and daughters, as both kin *and* strangers, insiders *and* outsiders in the theological academy. Exploring the complex condition of being black in America in the 1940s and '50s, Baldwin speaks as a native son, as one who can rightly claim himself as a citizen and inheritor of the American tradition, yet is treated as invisible and insignificant. Similarly, African Americans are nurtured inside of and contribute to theological contexts that nevertheless treat them as marginal and peripheral, pointing to the perpetual contradictions experienced by blacks in theological institutions. I testify about my experiences of being a native daughter as a way not only to illuminate the forms of structural racism that continue to plague the theological academy but also to demonstrate how persons like me continue to make theological spaces creative, dynamic, and life-giving. The theological contributions and persistent experiences of structural injustice among native sons and daughters must be acknowledged for theological education to be released into more liberative futures. I hope readers will explore how the complex experiences of African Americans in the academy invite them to ponder what their moral investments will be in envisioning theological futures in ways that are not captive to old racist institutional hierarchies and theological systems, especially when those ideologies and practices engender structural harm.

As a way to highlight the struggles and contributions of native daughters and sons, I foreground important voices such as Zora Neale Hurtson, Lorraine Hansberry, Yvette Flunder, Mattie Moss Clark, Emilie Townes, Delores Williams, Katie Cannon, and others. I offer narratives about my own theological formation and how it has shaped what I believe theological education is *and* can be. Chapter 1 offers the reader a glimpse into how the Afro-Pentecostal tradition shaped me in my early years and how I engaged important theological questions during my twenties within primarily white theological contexts. Chapters 2 and 3 look at white and black theological contexts respectively and explore the problems of structural racism and hetero-patriarchy that plague black women and black queer persons who are students and professors within theological education. My goal is not only to present the plight of black people within these structures (especially black women and black queer folk) but also to show how such spaces repress *and* affirm the gifts and talents of native daughters like myself within the academy. It is this insider/ outsider experience that I hope to capture in talking about the complex experiences of black persons in the academy.

The final chapter proposes one way to look toward the future of theological education by taking the experiences and contributions of native daughters and sons seriously. Here I attempt to *prophesy*, to offer a word about the future of theological education. I believe that we must be witnesses to a different theological formation by considering the contributions of progressive black Pentecostal communities and broader radical social movements, which are envisioning otherwise communities of intimacy and belonging. We must work not only for just structures and institutions; we must also imagine new ecologies of theological formation in which desires for caring and compassionate communities are truly possible. Without a desire to forge patterns of intimacy and belonging within community, we are lost.

A final comment about this book. I recognize that I am offering "notes" on what is fundamentally an oral tradition. Testifying *is* spoken word, uttered with and for community. This text might feel like a performative contradiction, forcing an oral tradition and collective mode of speech into a potentially closed form such as writing. Writing, unlike communal speech, is a largely solitary enterprise and endeavor, which risks distorting the power of testifying as a collective practice. This is a fair criticism. However, there is another way of viewing my intention: to foreground this oral tradition as central to theological education's transformation. Writing about this oral tradition honors this practice and my church community, presenting this mode of speech as a powerful form of knowledge in transforming the purposes and ends of theological education.

To capture my intention, I write in a loose form, in the form of meditations, stories, prayers, and lamentations to capture the fluid, dynamic nature of testifying. I capture all this not in the form of philosophical argumentation but in the form of "notes," a genre open to fluidity and diversity. Notes can come in many genres of writing, such as lists, jottings, lyrics to songs, favorite phrases, drawings, and so much more. Similar to notes, testifying does not adhere to some predetermined rational structure but makes pronouncements in ways that are creative, unpredictable, and deeply unconfined by conventional methods. Notes invite democratic ways of being. I offer an imperfect way of capturing this oral tradition of testifying in hopes that it will be used as a resource in thinking creatively about the present and futures of theological education.

In the following pages, the testimonies I offer may shock and surprise, offend and encourage, incite and inspire. From the emotional burdens black students and faculty endure by working under the duress of structural racism to rethinking how creative transformation can happen in theological education, I insist that we must linger with the words and testimonies of African Americans within theological education. I pray that my words call African Americans to testify and the broader theological academy to listen.

1

Hanging New Ornaments

A small gray church sits on a corner lot on Brown Street in my hometown. This small church is a sturdy building of gray bricks, black-paned windows, and two small entrance doors. It sits surrounded by deep luscious green grass, a place where we played many touch-tag games and ran marathons as children. To the east of the church once lay a gravel parking lot where families would get out of cars three to four times a week to participate in worship services and many kinds of rehearsals.

As a child, I would often stand on the porch of the church and look out into the neighborhood. Town residents called this neighborhood the "east side," which was the code phrase for the black community in Springfield, Illinois. But not just any black community: the ghetto. This phrase evoked the side of town that was rough, uncultured, and poor. It was a place middle-class people avoided if they could, an area of town where few white people congregated or fellowshiped. But this was our home, our spiritual mecca, the place where we came to experience a different kind of wealth, the wealth of love and joy cultivated within the deep bonds of community. We were joyful and lived inside of this joy. Our little gray church was where God was found and where we found God in each other.

This modest building reflected the people that it held. We were a congregation of sixty to one hundred people who entered the double doors leading into the sanctuary to beat our tambourines, to sing long songs that were marked by a call-and-response format, and to respond to the preached word with loud "Hallelujahs" and "Amens." Our time together in the sanctuary was loud, sensual, and unapologetically frenzied. That sacred time together was found not only in the sanctuary; it was found especially in the basement. The basement of the church is where we broke bread and laughed at the top of our lungs. The basement encouraged us to find God in the elements of bread and water, fried chicken and punch. Despite the austere look of the basement, we always took the time to decorate the tables with flowers, colorful paper plates, and plastic cups. This infusion of care into our eating together communicated the importance and sacredness of the body. Hunger was sinful if we could meet this need. And for those members who struggled to put food on the table, these meals marked their experience of salvation, a movable feast and eucharistic celebration. The saving grace of being fed a wonderful meal when uncertain where the next meal was coming from was a pure gift and another form of worship.

A place that birthed dozens of pastors, this small church house was the beginning of my memories of God, of stories, of community, of church mothers robed in white. The mothers' board had its own section of the church, perched right by the organ. These women were fierce and demanding. Clutching their purses in one hand and their Bibles in the other, these women knew struggle. As young black women in the 1930s and 1940s, they had experienced social and economic obstacles, even in the North, that can be difficult to imagine now. Although Illinois was not a part of the Jim Crow South, there was certainly informal segregation, disclosed in silent covenants and exclusive white-only eating clubs sustained by the whispered agreements of the white gentry. These women were no strangers to racial prejudice and discrimination. Many of them served as nurses and domestics. While broader white society may not have cherished them, our church gave them seats of honor at the front of the church, where everyone viewed them as God's daughters and mothers of Zion on whom the community depended.

The elders of the church may have occupied the pulpit (which was seen as a privileged space that could only be occupied by men), but these men depended on the wisdom and authority of the church mothers. I remember numerous occasions on which the church mothers openly rebuked an elder for disrespect or other infractions. These women were far from subjects to patriarchy, although later in this chapter I will nuance and complexify how the patriarchal structures of my childhood tradition impeded women who desired to be in ministry in unorthodox ways. Taking their cue from the church mothers, these elders were bold and claimed with exuberance and urgency that the Lord was with us, that God was on our side. I especially remember the elders inviting us as children to read the lesson books for Sunday school and midweek Bible study. I was truly excited to have such a central place in the worship service by reading aloud to the entire congregation. I felt special. It was only later that I discovered that some of the elders and church mothers were not literate (or could not read well). Yet many of them knew the Bible better than those members who could read.

My community had a powerful oral tradition of passing on both stories from the Bible and stories of how our ancestors trusted in the God of those stories. This oral tradition created church leaders who painted on the canvas of our hearts a hopeful picture of God's loving, compassionate nature. We learned a knowledge of the heart, of being with and for each other on this journey we call life. We knew it was the *quality* of our relationships within this community that bound us to practicing God's nature of love and care. We were not alone: we had each other.

With my community, my experience of crying out in ecstatic utterance invoked in me a desire to inch toward divine mysteries. Yet, this search for divine mystery and presence was one we carried in our *bodies*, not in rigid and abstract philosophical precepts. Our bodies and not only our minds were sites of divine knowledge. From the first moment we walked through the church doors, our experience was a deeply embodied experience. We met the first song with exuberant clapping and stomping. Sometimes, depending on how many of us were in the church, we could feel the church floor shaking as we danced and expressed God's ongoing movement and power in and through our bodies. When the choir sang, most people were on their feet, moving and swaying to the music.

There was a time for dancing or what we called "shouting," or what W. E. B. Du Bois referred to as "the frenzy." This time of dancing would often go on longer than the actual sermon. Sometimes, dancing could end up *being* the sermon. We rarely had printed programs as I was growing up, but if we did, the program would always have an asterisk at the top with this statement: "Program subject to change through the leading of the Spirit." We believed that the dance was indeed a primary vehicle through which to experience God's power, deliverance, intervention, and providence. The body was not just a bystander while the mind contemplated God. Rather, the body was active and often led the mind to an experience of God.

And *if* we made it to the sermon, the sermon was likewise a highly embodied activity. As the pastor forcefully preached the sermon, the congregation responded not only through verbal cues of affirmation such as "Amen!" Some congregants stood up on their feet and talked back to the pastor. Some congregants waved their hands in the air over and over, only to bring their hands back into a body hug and groan. Some congregants walked the aisles, shaking their heads, before returning to their seats. Most interestingly, some congregants could be so touched by the sermon that they disrupted the entire preached message, flowing into the aisles in order to dance and shout—but *only* when the music began.

Ah, the music! The music was legendary in our church. It is often said that the organ preaches the sermon *with* the black preacher. Certainly the organ holds a sacred place in the black church, particularly within the black Pentecostal worship experience. The music can often upstage the preacher, and one sensed a fight behind closed doors between pastor and organist. Often in the middle or at the end of a preacher's message, the organ begins to croon as background to the preacher's words, offering a dramatic, staccato-like flair to the preacher's words and statements. "God will pick you up" (organ plays dramatically), "turn you around" (organ plays even more dramatically), "place your feet on solid ground!" (organ shifts to high-pitched sounds and is loud and dramatic as if to punctuate the ending of an exclamatory sentence). In that moment, the presence and power of God sweep us away. Our bodies tremble. We experience God.

* * *

When I entered junior high, I became more aware of the importance of stories. My spiritual journey began with biblical stories that I heard my grandmother talk about in her living room or with her friends at Hardee's Restaurant. I would lean in to the stories told in Sunday school class or stories recounted by my pastor, Claude Farlow, who was a master storyteller. These stories were about biblical characters who were always "counted out," persons perpetually underestimated. Yet these characters had something stronger than societal expectations: they had God.

Exodus was a dominant narrative retold in my church, and a teacher or preacher would often belt out in a loud voice, "If God can deliver the children of Israel from bondage out of Egypt, God can deliver you from any of your issues!" In part, the fabled "Egyptland" described a state of spiritual bondage and existential hardship, a place where one sought to be delivered from spiritual wandering and restlessness. Those in my congregation often testified about their restless wanderings as pilgrims on the road of life seeking spiritual refuge. During testimony service, each of us would speak about our own personal spiritual wandering and how we overcame. Each week presented a new wilderness, a new opportunity to find communion and spiritual rest through our wrestlings with God. We supported each other through corporate prayer, whether we were gathered at the church or at someone's home.

For us, prayer was warfare. It was warfare until we took our last breath. Such prayer was about communicating our longings, actual attitudes, and convictions while facing down the finitude of our existence. Prayer was about the presence of God. And moving into the presence of God was hard work. It involved daily facing both our human possibilities and our limitations, those inclinations that inhibited us from actualizing ourselves as joyful, loving, and compassionate beings. Prayer allowed the tides of life to wash over our pain and sorrow, as we stretched our eyes toward the shores of joy and peace. This was a collective quest, a corporate pilgrimage to attain with our hearts what even money cannot buy.

Yet Egyptland also entailed the material persecutions that people within my congregation endured. Because my congregation struggled with underemployment and unemployment, one would constantly hear people refer to this nation as less than an "American dream." It wasn't that my community uncritically dismissed a number of benefits associated with this country; my community simply endured experiences that demonstrated a constant denial of these benefits to black people. We were Leah's children, not the preferred children of Jacob's beloved Rachel. Historically, black people have been dehumanized, despised, and simply unloved within a society that never meant to value such lives above mere commoditization. This history has material consequences. I could see it etched in the faces of many in our congregation. I heard feelings of material uncertainty reinforced by institutions that did little to remedy past and present racial injustices and aggressions. They lamented being systematically locked out of simply having *enough*.

While I lived a middle-class existence, the economic suffering of others within our congregation left an indelible imprint on my psyche. They needed social respect. They needed to be *heard* and *seen* truly. Despite these hardships, my community was resilient. In fact, part of our pilgrimage was to embody resilience in the face of uncertainty and material insecurity. My community at Brown Street moved and inspired me to reflect on how my faith illuminated the dark places of society.

Given those persistent dark places, we were always cultivating experiences of communal joy and hope. Another of my absolute favorite biblical stories was that of Pentecost in the book of Acts, and it was always the most dramatically staged story in our church. The first announcement that we were entering the sacred terrain of retelling Pentecost often began with the words "And they were gathered together in one accord." This is a verse right out of the Acts narrative, a line that signals what was held as sacred within our community: our joyful togetherness, our unbreakable bond of living and loving each other. We were of one accord.

Pentecost was of ultimate importance to my community because the Acts community spoke with tongues of fire. Fire was an important metaphor to my community, and no wonder: God appears to Moses in a burning bush. God led the children of Israel in a pillar of cloud by day and a pillar of fire by night to give them light. John the Baptist says of Jesus that he will come to baptize us with the Holy Spirit and fire. The writer of Hebrews talks of God as a consuming fire. We danced, shouted, and cried out to God with passion that was consuming like fire. We understood fire not just as destructive but as a source for heat, protection, light, and purification. It was this fire we talked about, searched for, and, once experienced, testified about in celebration of new life. I too wanted to experience God as fire.

Pentecost was also about the *miraculous* for my community. The miraculous was a necessary experience that defies the *status quo and its logic*, breaking open *impossible* spiritual possibilities for flourishing together. The miraculous is highly disruptive of the order of things, the logic of this order. Just imagine: the disciples gather in the upper room in Jerusalem, waiting, as instructed by the resurrected Christ, to receive the Holy Spirit. Then something happens that they do not expect or even desire. They speak in tongues, in the native languages of Jews gathered from around the world. This must have been shocking and unexpected. It was certainly disruptive. The gathered Jews hear the disciples in their own native languages and are stupefied. They ask, "What does this mean?" They are lost for words and quite confused. Clearly, the impossible is transpiring. But they cannot deny what they hear: *something that was impossible is now possible.* None of the disciples in the upper room could have known the mother languages of Jews living in Asia, Egypt, and other places. For the disciples to have known these mother tongues, they would have had to travel to these places, study these languages with natives of the area in a slow and meticulous way, and learn the culture and politics out of which the language emerges. The disciples had not done that. So, again, the gathered crowds are left wondering how this is *possible.* As theologian Willie Jennings concludes, this event is *purely an act of the Spirit.*[1] Pentecost is grounded in the language of miracles. The impossible becomes possible through the work of the Spirit.

Jennings most importantly names the true miracle of Pentecost as described in the book of Acts: the miracle of revolutionary intimacy.[2] Language is about identity, community, and intimacy. To know and speak someone's language, particularly when that person is from far away, is to create an intimacy in the encounter between you and the native speaker. The power of Pentecost is the Spirit's announcement of *revolutionary intimacy:* this is what the Spirit would create in this new community after Pentecost. In a world that did not desire intimacy across differences, this new community of Jesus's followers would constitute a community marked by revolutionary intimacy. This revolutionary intimacy would not be intimacy according to tribal or nationalistic boundaries. This community would disrupt these boundaries, uniting unlikely people through desires for intimacy and belonging. This kind of community could only be the work of the Spirit.

My Pentecostal community spoke in the language of miracles. Although early Pentecostalism as seen in the Azusa Street Revival of 1906 briefly exemplified this revolutionary intimacy across differences, much of contemporary Pentecostalism has focused less on this practice. Nevertheless, Pentecost was important for my religious community, as it disrupted the logics and orders of this world, a world often driven by gross inequities of power.

I was a believer in the miraculous. And I wanted this fire. From a young age, I would climb the steps of our small gray church in order to kneel down at the altar. I was on a quest. When I was not at the church altar, I was in front of the altar I had constructed in my room, right on top of my hamper. Decorating this altar with books and cloth was my way to reach divine presence, a way to communicate my longings and my desires to experience this consuming, disruptive presence.

* * *

Like all testimonies, mine also contains pain, trauma, and loss. A few turning points reshaped my spiritual journey and eventually my theological quest. The first was more of a gradual experience, an awakening from a deep slumber. It was my unfolding awareness of how racism is covertly exercised in my hometown, a town that ironically prides itself on being the home of Abe Lincoln, the Great Emancipator. That awareness came chiefly through the predominantly white private academy where I was educated. If only the halls could speak! So many black students talked to each other about the micro-aggressions they experienced within this school context. For all the virtues of this private academy (and there are many), the white community associated with this academy fundamentally saw itself as color-blind, even as postracial, which created a deep frustration in many students of color who attended.

It is for such reasons that I have a complex relationship with this academy. While I was deeply affirmed there, many other students of color felt differently and have a hard time returning to the school. Conversations about how structural racism sits inside such institutions have been nonexistent. In fact, to suggest that racial problems are present is to be seen as a troublemaker in such communities. I remember that as a student I desperately wanted to ask school authorities: Have you ever sat down with black students and guaranteed them freedom to speak without fear of reprimand? Have you ever asked such questions of them—and listened?

I do remember being asked about the problem of racism, but it was after I had graduated high school. I visited my hometown over Christmas break during my first year of college and decided to drop by my former school. While I was chatting with a white male administrator, he asked me a question about black history and racism. He mentioned that some African American parents wanted the school to be more invested in teaching the history of racism in the United States. These parents felt that part of the spiritual and moral formation of their children (and all the children in the school) involved understanding the black history and moral entanglements of this country. Understandably, these parents believed that their children needed this kind of moral support from the academy. After offering this background, the male administrator looked me in the eyes and asked, "Should we talk about the history of racism here?" We stood there in complete silence. I stood there silently not so much because of the question but because of the tone of the question, a tone that invited a specific answer, one that would affirm his bias. This tone made me feel like a high school student all over again, wondering whether to respond at all.

I remember fear and shame creeping across my body after I offered this two-word response: "Not necessarily." When I said this, the administrator immediately jumped in, affirming that it is indeed not wise to revisit the past. The past is the past, after all, right? He continued by claiming that racism was after all not an experience at this academy and therefore did not need to be engaged. I stood there silently, partly nodding my head, eager to change the subject. I felt so ashamed—not only in this moment but also long after this encounter—for being unwilling to speak my truth.

It was only years later that I realized what had transpired. Growing up in this academy, I still felt I could be penalized for saying something that implicated this school, that called out why this administrator and the broader school neglected to engage the very real racial pain and trauma that students of color experience in its halls and classrooms. I left heartbroken, blaming myself for how the conversation had gone. Only now do I know that my feelings of fear reflect a broader reality of white privilege, a privilege that presumes to have all the answers before the question has been posed. This is what I felt that day, and it became the impetus for me moving forward always to speak the truth to white communities.

The past is not simply the past; it continues to encroach upon the present. My younger brother's experience would also demonstrate the power of the past at this school. One day, my younger brother and a few of his black friends found a noose tied to the basketball hoop in the gym. My mother called me that evening enraged. I could hear devastation in my younger brother's voice, and anger. The administrator who knew about this event initially had done nothing in response (although a higher-up administrator eventually addressed it). And my mind went back to the conversation I had had with this white male administrator about racial and racist actions not being part of this academy. He was so very wrong. And my brother's pain and trauma were proof of that. I subsequently watched my brother fail to thrive in this school context. It wasn't until he went to college and found mentors that he began to blossom, finding his voice and vocation as a young black man.

Similar to this academy, a number of white leaders in my hometown of Springfield see themselves as color-blind, as exemplars of Lincoln's party.[3] They are unable to talk about histories of informal Jim Crow in their own communities because they understand Springfield as exemplifying the opposite of Southern racism. But of course, Northern cities played a significant role in reproducing racial domination in America. And Northern universities shared in this work. In *Ebony and Ivy*, Craig Steven Wilder recounts how the earliest institutions of higher education in the United States built their wealth from the enslavement of Africans and the subjugation of Native Americans. For instance, Wilder notes that Dartmouth College depended upon African slave labor during its early years in two ways. First, the college depended upon wealthy Southern donors to contribute to the college's largesse. Academic administrators found themselves courting benefactors whose money was attached to Southern slave plantation economies. Second, people enslaved by the college outnumbered faculty, administrators, and active trustees, as the enslaved were used as free labor in the building of every material aspect related to college life.[4] Faculty often owned slaves who were allowed to migrate from the South to such universities for this express purpose. The slave economy and the rise of university education were intertwined, feeding off each other to generate massive wealth for the United States.

This history of cities in the "North" (any state that was not "South") belies these Northern cities being simply the antithesis of their backward Southern counterparts. Any true version of Springfield's story remembers the city's role in the reproduction of white supremacy. Yet this narrative is repressed and silenced in order to maintain an ideological myth. For if Springfield is postracial, race cannot be named as a problem. Consequently, race and racism are conversations that can never really be voiced. Near the end of my high school years, I realized that my sense of Christian faith needed to acknowledge these realities and respond to them.

The next turning point in my life felt more like a collision. I was twelve years old. I attended a jurisdictional service (comprised of about twenty-five to thirty-five churches) in my denomination, a special service that elicited excitement and elation in many in the city. I remember talking about this event for four entire weeks leading up to the actual service. Because Springfield is rather small and uneventful, any special occasion sent us out into the shopping malls to buy new dresses, hats, shoes, purses, jewelry, and more.

This service welcomed a major gospel singer to preach. Her name was Dorinda Clark Cole, a famous singer who was most known by her role in the Clark Sisters, a gospel group comprised of five sisters who changed the sound of gospel music. The Clark Sisters were gospel royalty, trained by their mother, Dr. Mattie Moss Clark. Dr. Mattie was a famous traditional gospel singer in her own right. She was born in Alabama, and her mother was a musician, preacher, and bishop herself. Music was required in her home, and by the time she was an adult, she played multiple instruments. Mattie was a composer of music, recording more than one hundred gospel songs. In light of her being a gospel music success around the world, she was called upon to train choirs in my denomination, eventually becoming the International Music President in Church of God in Christ (COGIC). Great gospel composers and musicians such as Walter Hawkins and James Moore would be deeply influenced and shaped by her musical genius.

Dr. Mattie was a sight to behold. She would mount the stage clothed in a gorgeous flowing robe. Most black Pentecostals would never have the opportunity to sing with an award-winning orchestra or choir, but Dr. Mattie walked onto the stage like an orchestra conductor, emanating affirmation and confidence that these choir members were about to sing heaven down. The choir imbibed this confidence, and as her directing gestures guided the musical pulse and rhythms of the singers and musicians, three-part harmony sounds entered the air, providing spiritual inspiration. These sounds swept over the hearts of those in the room. I remember a top gospel hit she composed, "Climbing Up the Mountain," which was filled with fast-paced singing that encouraged the saints to finish their journey of faith with trust in God. The journey would not be easy, it reminded us, as climbing mountains takes determination and grit. My childhood church sang this song almost every other Sunday. We were definitely compelled by the musical witness Dr. Mattie shared with us.

Her excellence in music was paired with her no-nonsense disposition. I would hear stories about her short temper when choir members assumed that gospel music was simply about passion and earthiness. For her, it was also about musical precision. If a singer was musically imprecise, that singer would likely encounter the full force of Dr. Mattie's personality. Her presence was exacting and demanding, bold and blunt when one did not rise to the occasion and manifest the power, beauty, and precision of gospel music. One legendary story about her revolves around her daughter "Twinkie" Clark, who, upon playing the wrong notes on the organ as an adult while at a large conference, was escorted right off the organ. Dr. Mattie did not play around. And she brought this rigor to her daughters, training their voices and introducing them to the recording world. Dr. Mattie evoked both admiration and fear. For better or worse, this was who she was. She became one of the most noted and admired gospel musicians and Pentecostal preachers of the twentieth century.

Even more amazing, Dr. Mattie incarnated the black preaching style. In 1983 at the COGIC Women's Convention, she preached a sermon entitled "No Escape and No Excuse," reminding the attendees to offer no excuses in living a righteous, Christian life. At the end of her message, she performed her version of a traditional black preaching "celebration." The organ began playing, accompanying her words of proclamation. She and the organ became one, and she started to "speak-sing" words of encouragement: "Wash me, Lord, until my hands look new; wash me, Lord, until my feet look new. Wash me!" The crowd responded, "Wash me!" Although only men were seen as being able to preach like this in our denomination, she proved that she was master of them all.[5]

Of course, greatness would mark her girls. She had plans for them. Building on their mother's legacy, the Clark Sisters embodied a new kind of musical world that combined traditional gospel, urban beats, jazz, and blues, all mixed together to form a masterful musical style. Winners of three Grammys, these women were known for their perfect pitch, for close harmony, and most of all, for popularizing forms of scat singing within Pentecostal churches. When attending my denomination's Holy Convocation each year as a child, I would sit on the edge of my seat and wait to hear the remarkable singing virtuosity of these sisters. Hearing them sing was like watching a volcano erupt and overflow into every open space below. Listening to these women moved hearts and enraptured bodies. It made us jump to our feet, wave our hands, shout out loud, "You betta sing!" to these priestesses of high praise. Their voices transported us to a place of new birth, feeling a new sense of awe and wonder at the power of sound to make the body and spirit whole.

Dorinda was unique because she was the sister who could sing *and* preach. She was Dr. Mattie all over again. I remember the first time I heard her: it was in my living room watching a VHS tape of her preaching. I was enthralled. She was elegant and possessed an untouchable quality that inspired me as a small girl child. I sat there in front of the TV and didn't move. I wanted to catch every word, every move, every musical break she performed near the end of her sermon. I wanted to soak in her example. I was now a Dorinda Clark Cole fan. Her singing was great, but it was her preaching that made me her disciple.

So I was awaiting her arrival with elation, along with much of the community. I clearly remember sitting in the second row in the church. She entered the sanctuary from the side. I held my breath. I watched as a pastor led her up the side aisle to my right and escorted her up to the pulpit. I was stunned. My concentration on her broke completely as I sat in disbelief at what I was seeing: a woman preacher being escorted to sit in the *pulpit*. For certain, she deserved to sit in the pulpit. But this wasn't the cognitive dissonance my twelve-year-old mind was experiencing in this moment. I was stunned because my denomination taught us that the pulpit was reserved only for men who preached the gospel. Women could "teach" but never "preach," and they did that teaching from the floor. The space of the pulpit was a sacred area that was highly gendered, marking a masculinist ideal of church polity and leadership. With absolute conviction, we were taught that men as purveyors of the preached word were to occupy the pulpit space, the holy lectern. This was a spiritual truth for my denomination—at least that is the way it was taught.

But here I was, watching Dorinda be escorted into the pulpit and seated by pastors who had preached this gospel of pulpit segregation for decades. There she was, standing and preaching in the pulpit, a space denied to women in my hometown simply for being women. I honestly don't remember her sermon. I sat there transfixed, pondering: What did this moment *mean*? It was a new moment in terms of gender representation in the pulpit within my mind. Next, I wondered: Could *I* do this? Would *I* be welcomed with open arms to the pulpit if I ever desired to *preach*? Were other women that evening experiencing the same tension? I had too many questions and too few answers. Although I did not have the vocabulary to express what was transpiring in my mind and heart, that evening marked a critical turning point for me. I became a questioner, what today in theological education we would call a critical thinker of my "inherited traditions."

Even though I was only twelve, I immediately grasped that Dorinda Clark Cole was famous and rich, an upper-class black woman with tremendous potential to make churches profitable or accrue social capital through her presence. The many women who served daily within these local churches, most of them working-class women, were simply not given similar consideration. Could it be that a venerated tradition can be broken only if one has sufficient class status? The economics of this decision became evident as I reflected on this moment for about two weeks. I remember attempting to follow up with my family members to express my confusion. I asked: Why was Dorinda to be privileged above the women that make these ministries possible? But I received no real answers. It wasn't so much that my family members were trying to dismiss my questions as that they recognized the flagrant contradictions of that evening and simply wanted my twelve-year-old mind to release itself from the burden of pondering questions about actions that were overtly hypocritical.

This moment caused me to question my childhood view of religious hierarchy and authority. Indeed, I became the queen of questions. I had been taught to accept and defend what the community believed and that questioning was not only a form of disbelief but most importantly a form of disrespect toward God. Now I wondered: Was questioning a form of *belief*? Couldn't doubt be a sign of faith? In that moment, doubt was less about sin and more about taking seriously what I held as most sacred— my spiritual beliefs—and how I made sense at a young age of the world through my faith. Questioning was a door that opened into something different, a difference that I knew intuitively would change my twelve-year-old life, although I could not anticipate then just how profoundly this spiritual disposition of questioning would transform me.

A final turning point was the general terror that I constantly felt of the rigid, legalistic dimensions of my childhood Pentecostal faith. While my church community was profoundly caring, it was also incredibly judgmental. Persistent conversations about what one could *not* do overwhelmed my young mind and heart. The measure of one's salvation, my community insisted, was directly related to whether the rules were followed. These "rules" were about the mandate to live a sanctified life. When I was growing up in my tradition, sanctification was considered an outward act of personal piety that involved an entire symbolic system. For my community, outward symbols, such as women wearing long skirts and no makeup, constituted what it meant to lead a holy and sanctified life. What it meant to be righteous was bound up with symbolic acts such as not wearing shorts, abstaining from alcohol, staying away from movie theaters, and refusing to dance to "worldly" music (nongospel music). I was constantly on edge, waiting for my sins to catch up with me. Consequently, I remember being constantly unsure of my salvation as a young teenager and then a young adult. Fear oftentimes drove my form of faith, as my image of God was of One who was stern, wrathful, and harsh.

Of particular concern to sanctification was the disciplining of the body. Everything was focused on the body, particularly what one did *with* the body. Although the word was rarely mentioned publicly, sex was the litmus test for one's salvation. The face of sin was lust, especially lust of the flesh. I was taught to suppress my urgings and pray them away. Although I later discovered that only through responsibly engaging one's sexual urgings can one live an honest and authentic life, my sense of sexuality was severely repressed as a young woman, rooted in my tradition's refusal to engage forms of desire honestly, including sexual desire. When I speak of my community's inability to engage conversations about desire honestly, I am referring to the gap between what was taught and what people were actually living out. So many members were having sex outside of traditional marriage—in their houses, in other people's houses, even in church basements. Every year, new scandals emerged that were met with intentional silence, as parents concealed their children's sexual infractions or clergymen were once again forgiven for their sexual misconduct.

What was most interesting about my community was the silence that surrounded identity and sexuality. We had a number of gay members who led various ministries in our churches and relied on a "don't ask, don't tell" policy. Some of the men conformed to the church's norms for expressions of gender and sexuality, at least in public. But others resisted these norms, working their long choir robes like Broadway divas. However, clergy leaders overlooked these issues of gender identity and performance. As long as these men contributed to the Sunday morning worship and kept their mouths shut about who they really were, all would be well. Something about this way of living seemed dishonest and inauthentic. I knew I could not live like that.

I said very little to those around me as I held my many questions close to my heart. However, I had a cousin, Eddie, who one day started a conversation with me about life, faith, and love. I was in high school. I opened up. Now, I must admit that Eddie was brilliant, fun loving, witty, and *irreverent*. He was an out gay black man in the 1980s and '90s, a pretty difficult role to play within the Pentecostal community in which we were raised. Eddie had some problems that made him an undesirable conversation partner on faith to most in my family. However, I found conversation with him to be a gift. This is important because my family was filled with preachers, pastors, and worship leaders. Yet, I found reprieve *with him*. We talked about everything, and I could bring my questions to our conversations without encountering judgment from him. He taught me compassion, and he taught me how to listen to my own thoughts, to truly honor the musings of my own heart.

I discovered that questions and conversation are signs of faith. Questions help us to recognize what we value most, how such questioning is about honoring the significance of that which is being questioned. I felt particles of strength grow around me as I leaned into writing and journaling about my questions, about things that didn't quite make sense to me, beliefs that deep down seemed inauthentic to my experiences. I also learned that questioning reshapes and remakes one's ideas *and* one's ways of being. I felt I was being remade and rebirthed. I felt pure joy.

* * *

I became an independent thinker while in college. I know that is incredibly predictable, as so many young people start to think for themselves at this stage in life. Yet my unfolding was somewhat different. My process toward conscientization was a slow boil, like a simmer that evolves into an eruption. I was clear that my growing feminist sensibilities occupied a liminal space, an in-betweenness, that did not want to choose between being religious and being "feminist." On the one hand, to be religious within my Pentecostal tradition meant to reject secular or "worldly" philosophies like feminism, as my tradition interpreted these ideas not only as antibiblical but also as antiblack (meaning against black men and the nuclear black family). On the other hand, some feminist texts I read while in college implicitly gestured toward the feminist and religious as incommensurable discourses. I was stuck. I needed a feminism that affirmed my deep religiosity. I spent the majority of my college life secretly reading classical feminist and black feminist texts that the fields of political philosophy and literature introduced to me, a significant memory I elaborate further in chapter 3. I felt a double bind, as I kept my feminist questions and religious ideas separate, although they were already merging into each other as the shore merges into the ocean.

That all changed in 2004. I met her at Yale. I was a student working on my master's in religion and ethics. She was fierce and unapologetically black. She had already written several books on womanist theology and ethics, probing the interconnections between spirituality, black women, and the quest for social justice. She was one of the teachers that changed the course of my life. Dr. Emilie Townes was incredibly accomplished but never paraded her success. She didn't have to. Her presence was like a quiet storm. She was a womanist and a scholar who married theological reflection with critiques of systems of power, systems that created racial, gender, class, and sexual disparities. I was taken by the breadth and depth of her knowledge *and* by her kindness as a master pedagogue. Her teaching style was infused with conversations on Maria Stewart, Frederick Douglass, Barbara Jordan, Katie Cannon, and more. Her teaching expressed a commitment to helping us students investigate the racist, hetero-patriarchal, and classed structures that continue to plague our society and religious institutions (such as churches).

Her class was like an exit that you hadn't known existed off of a familiar highway. This exit transported me to new intellectual terrain that opened up to an endless horizon of new adventures and possibilities. What captured my mind and heart was that she introduced me to black women thinkers who married black feminist and womanist sensibilities with the religious. I read works by Kelly Brown Douglas and Marcia Riggs, black women scholars who reconstructed religious perspectives through their attention to the lives of black women. These thinkers did not see the religious and feminist and womanist as mutually exclusive but as mutually inclusive, as a way to fashion liberatory practices oriented toward black flourishing. This was important, for I needed to find a way to speak faithfully yet critically about my own burgeoning theological questions. My questions needed to be engaged within the context of the academy, churches, and broader society.

I did wrestle with the fact that this kind of religious awakening came to full voice at Yale, within a predominantly white institution (PWI). What would it mean to critique the black church contexts from which I came by appealing to the theological education I received at an elite white institution like Yale? For certain, Townes as a black voice affected me in a major way at Yale, but it would be intellectually dishonest not also to acknowledge the invaluable ways that Miroslav Volf and Margaret Farley shaped me. Volf, the child of a Pentecostal pastor and now an internationally renowned theologian, was the first professor at Yale to encourage me to pursue doctoral studies. I remember feeling unsure about doctoral work, coming from a social science undergraduate background, but he explicitly told me I could do it. I also found myself inspired not simply by what he said but also by how he moved through the world of theological education as someone who came out of a Pentecostal tradition. Though not a black woman, he was a mentor nevertheless. I could relate to him because I understood the complex journey from such Pentecostal beginnings. Similarly, Farley was a white Catholic nun and feminist scholar at Yale who took me under her intellectual wing. I learned womanism and African religious feminisms from her, eventually meeting African feminist theologian Mercy Amba Oduyoye while at Yale. Even then, I wrestled with what it means to be native daughter, what it means to learn and grow from a diversity of mentors within the very institutional contexts that affirm and repress people like me.

Another memorable moment at Yale was my introduction to Zora Neale Hurston's *The Sanctified Church*. I took an independent study with Farley on Hurston that changed my life. I was struck by Hurston's fidelity to dignifying black forms of cultural and religious expression that others dismissed as primitive and even demonic. Her thick descriptions of the religious rituals and practices of community making of the sanctified church helped me to interpret my own Pentecostal community. Similar to the time when Hurston was writing, the educated black elite of today often see the "frenzied" practices of charismatic and Pentecostal communities as emotive, irrational, and escapist. Hurston confronted and dismantled these stereotypes associated with the sanctified church. In this compilation of essays, she renarrates "sanctified folk" away from the European standards that judged such people as crude and absurd.

Of great importance is how Hurston situated the sanctified community: as creators and purveyors of spiritual knowledge. This community participated in the creation of religious knowledge in and through their performative experiences of the divine. Hurston elucidated this religious community's acts of knowledge creation as "original." What is interesting about her claim of originality is not that she was trying to speak of sanctified experiences as some kind of "return to the source" in the sense that these experiences are authentic and more "black" because of their connection to slave religious practices. Rather, she wanted to reject European and black middle-class evaluations of sanctified religious expression in which the religious practices and rituals of the sanctified world are described as wild, uncouth, and base. For Hurston, these valuations fostered "self-despisement" in middle-class blacks who distinguish themselves from the savage blackness of sanctified black communities, which were disproportionately constituted by lower-class blacks.[6] Hurston wanted to disrupt and rupture the problem of self-despisement among African Americans by turning to the complex and dynamic world of the sanctified church.

Hurston's essays describe the sanctified church as artistic. At these sanctified services, an individual who leads out in public prayer is empowered as the single speaker to "hang . . . new ornaments" upon the tradition of the collective community.[7] In this case, individual sanctified members possess artistic expression within a tradition that is highly malleable, supple, and open to new modes of being. As artists, sanctified folk create anew collective forms of religious expression to make meaning in the world. Speaking of the creative religious expression of the sanctified church as artistic, Hurston recovered the complex agency of these people and demonstrated the rich and variegated ways they move in the world to experience faith, joy, and transcendence.

I infer from Hurston that in order to understand the sanctified church, one must do what scholars refer to as "exegeting the congregation."[8] It means one cannot turn abstractly to church doctrines. One must be attentive to the congregation itself, as the meaning of practices is grounded in the subjective experiences and existential dilemmas of the congregation. One must inquire: Who really are these people, this congregation? Anthropologist Clifford Geertz reminds us that in order to interpret a culture, one must study the symbolic webs of significance that the community spins.[9] These webs of significance include the community's ritual acts, daily practices, rites of passage, sacred stories, and more. Such webs of significance generate and maintain the meanings and worldviews of the community. In fact, these webs of significance or worldviews offer cohesive narratives of existence, helping the community navigate the broader world in a way that leads to fulfillment and flourishing (whatever account of flourishing the community holds up as ideal).

One needs to understand these webs of significance to get behind the stories and mental maps of my small childhood community. Like Hurston, I have witnessed the deformations and distortions of observers who attempt to interpret my communities without considering their webs of significance. For example, simply interpreting vigorous dancing within Pentecostal communities as emotive and irrational ignores and dismisses how these religious communities experience divine presence, in and through their bodies. *Bodies mediate divine reality.* As I discussed earlier, the religious experience of Pentecostal communities is *somatic*, in that divine encounter happens through the flesh. This kind of religious experience cannot be interpreted through an overreliance on doctrines. While doctrinal confessions may factor in understanding the community's webs of significance, these worldviews and "mental maps" of meaning are more deeply rooted in the *bodily experience* of the divine, bodies that are in conversation with spiritual truths. Within my community, while a particular religious experience through the body can confirm a historical understanding of God, other religious experiences through the body can critique previously accepted "truths" or open up altogether new avenues of thought about God. In other words, such bodily experiences within different Pentecostal communities *create open-ended theological frameworks*. I believe Hurston wanted to capture this quality within the sanctified church through her writings. Those writings invited me to exegete the congregation. I felt invited to "hang new ornaments" on the Pentecostal tradition out of which I emerged, rather than dispensing completely with the tradition because of its significant problems.

Most important, exegeting the congregation is also about discerning and contemplating the community's potential future. For homiletics scholar Nora Tisdale, discovering the sacred stories out of which a community crafts a sense of identity unveils the "storied mirror" into which the congregation itself can look and truthfully see its own authentic reflection.[10] This storied mirror enables the community to see not only its remarkable traits of moral beauty but also its moral dishevelment. The community's ability to *see* such moral disorder sheds light on the community's future possibilities to be different, to occupy an alternative existential posture in the world.

This storied mirror can help the congregation to step outside of its old ways of seeing and being in order to embrace new creative possibilities. A congregation needs to understand and accept that certain stories, rituals, and practices no longer work, that these stories may even be morally ugly. In my tradition, such moral ugliness included its disregard for women by excluding women from top-tier levels of leadership. Although women certainly have always provided spiritual and moral leadership within my childhood denomination, as a matter of policy they were barred from occupying formal ecclesial positions such as pastor and elder. This policy of excluding women continues to affect the future possibilities of churches within my denomination. What might it mean to allow women to lead at all levels, empowering them to be decision makers within the institutional fabric of the denomination? The future possibilities of Pentecostal communities *hinge on women*. Gender parity in leadership and decision making then remains central to exploring creative possibilities. Hurston and Tisdale invite readers to critique and trust the inner workings and meaning making of sanctified traditions. As a seminary student of Farley, Volf, and Townes, I started doing precisely this.

* * *

These thinkers and mentors gave me a new *experience* of God. They allowed me to hang new ornaments. I did not want to abandon the God of my childhood. However, I did have questions about how my religious community interpreted God. Within my childhood church, God was loving and compassionate but also legalistic and unbendingly full of judgment and wrath. At times, my childhood faith was more about a strict way of moral living than about a deep authenticity rooted in the power of our beautiful yet fallible humanity. Being human and feeling the perpetual tug of one's finitude was hard to talk about in a tradition that truly believed one could transcend one's finitude by living a sinless existence. I remember being perpetually unsure and unsettled about my own eternal salvation as a high school and college student. This created profound spiritual unease and uncertainty in my young life.

After experiencing a different way of talking about the divine while in divinity school, I became more aware of my own embedded theological assumptions and ideas that closed me off to the many possibilities within the world. Being more open to new ways of being is incredibly important. For instance, while in college, it was hard for me to engage in a meaningful way with religious traditions other than Christianity and with people who possessed liberal views of sexuality. My childhood tradition had taught me to be suspicious and judgmental of people who did not think or believe as I did. If you could not convert them, you had to cease all fellowship with them. This zero-sum game had dire consequences for how I thought about people who differed from me and for how I formed relationships with others. After attending seminary, I found myself opening up my heart to new ways of seeing others. Seminary expanded my view of the world and others in it, making me a more compassionate expression of love and care. It helped me to embody a more humane way of being.

I developed what might be termed a "theology of the edge." Through my engagement with countercultural theological and social thinkers, I was moving toward a deeper understanding of Jesus's message and mission. I agree with theologian and religious leader Yvette Flunder that Jesus's mission must be considered in relation to the "edges" of society. These edges include those who are marginalized, silenced, tyrannized, and subjugated. Jesus didn't and doesn't just acknowledge these kinds of people, *he gathered and gathers them to form a radically inclusive community of love and justice.* I watch both society and church oftentimes fail to be attentive to the edges. In fact, those on the edge of society are seen as the problem. While my more conservative childhood tradition certainly attended to the edges of society, my community nevertheless had frozen views of truth, often believing they had a monopoly on God as they excluded people who differed from them. This disturbed me. I wanted a way to attend to the edges of society while being open to the *inadequacy* of my own ideas about God in the world.

Many liberal Christian communities may offer formal nods to those who occupy the fringes of society, but they *refuse to gather them in.* These liberal communities refuse to enter into authentic community with the poor or with people of color. Black same-gender-loving persons have described the insidious, covert racism they experience within white gay Christian communities. And while the poor are mentioned in the liturgy and theological proclamations of white and black liberal communities, the poor are rarely invited into such communities to speak and to participate fully in the common life of the congregation. How can liberal communities truly be in the vanguard against poverty if they have a hard time sitting next to homeless people on Sunday morning? While pastoring in a local church, I recall many parishioners complaining about the smell of some homeless people in the church pews. I wanted a theology of the edge that not only acknowledged the humanity of these children of God but also gathered them in to participate in authentic community.

This edge sensibility changed my view of God. God was less an unrelenting judge who was ready to punish me for the smallest infraction and more a God who gracefully invited me into an enlarged understanding of divine love, mutuality, and embrace. This edge sensibility requires vulnerability and humility toward people and ways of being that might be different from my own. My idea of the world and my place in it was beginning to expand.

With this edge sensibility, I fostered new experiences of God. These experiences were not just the high-pitched preaching and staccato-style musical notes that pervaded my childhood experiences. They also included following the questions I posed about the limitations of all I knew. Such experiences involved *holding new questions as forms of faith* as I sought to experience a new birth. This new birth was not in radical discontinuity with my childhood tradition, but it did disrupt ideas and practices that could no longer serve my sense of expanding possibilities. I found a way to place my persistent questions alongside my passion for my religious faith shaped out of community and struggle.

35

It was a new day for me. I knew that I was between two worlds that could not easily be reconciled, if they needed to be reconciled at all. But I knew one thing: whether in a classroom or in the sanctuary of my childhood church, God was present. God was with me. And hanging new ornaments on my tradition would be the profoundest of gifts.

2

Learning to Pass

Now that I am a tenured professor at Princeton Theological Seminary, an elite white Presbyterian institution whose endowment is larger than the financial resources of many countries, it *appears* that I have been able to crack the code of the academic career ladder, that I have become a winner in dominant white structures of theological education. I have, after all, experienced favorable reception of my intellectual and scholarly work in diverse institutional contexts, the theological guilds in particular and the humanities more broadly. I am participating in training doctoral students at Princeton, contributing to their process of formation within the theological academy. One might assume that I have been given complete access to elite realms of theological education and that I experience myself as inhabiting a position of authority.

These assumptions are mistaken, at least partially. Certainly, I benefit economically from elite structures within the theological context. However, as a black woman, I also experience a kind of loss that I describe as "learning to pass." In theological education, learning to pass means learning how to perform intellectual mastery within white institutions. It means mastering and teaching the white "normative" discourses and figures as well as those treated in more peripheral ways, without much choice in the matter. In theology, I am expected to master (or at least know well) Barth, but rarely are white students or professors required to master Cone or Gutiérrez. As a way to prove my academic prowess, I may be required to court major university publishers who might not even value the kind of scholarship I do. In learning to pass, I must step outside of what feels natural to me. In order to be "legible" within dominant modes, I must render myself intelligible within normative white standards of scholarship and teaching. Learning to pass (and the desire to pass) must be seen against the inequitable reality that scholars like myself often endure. We are celebrated if we render ourselves intelligible within popular or "rigorous" intellectual frames but are estranged and policed if we challenge dominant ways of doing "intellectual" work. Some scholars of color (such as black, Asian, Latinx) feel hostility within Eurocentric models and adjust themselves to this environment in order to stay afloat psychologically and emotionally.

Learning to pass is a reflexive response to a major dis-ease of theological education, which is the experience of intersectional forms of structural racism among black students and faculty, although such structural racism has not been officially documented by theological institutions like the Association of Theological Schools (ATS).[1] This dis-ease of theological education called *structural racism* manifests at the level of identity (*who* may speak on what properly constitutes theological education) and epistemology (*what* counts as theological knowledge). Learning to pass theologically is a central dilemma for African Americans (and people of color) in the theological academy, a dilemma to be exposed and resisted.

* * *

Learning to pass is a form of what Du Bois called double consciousness. As a person of color, you operate in a world that was not created for you, a world that has defined itself through categories that deny your humanity. Structural racism and its intersectional realities sit at the center of the theological academy's institutional life. Yet, this is a world that I attempt to make my own, even my home. And indeed, in part the theological academy *is* home, for it has been the context out of which I have been trained intellectually and theologically as a black woman. Moreover, black scholars have deeply shaped this home. I have embraced myself as a native daughter of this context, despite the diverse forms of structural racism that persist there. However, to be respected intellectually in the white spaces of theological education has entailed living an exilic existence, often leaving behind other aspects of my black and Pentecostal identity that do not conform neatly to methods and dispositions of intellectual rigor and soundness. I have had to exist in ways that feel fragmented and compartmentalized in order to demonstrate academic prowess. A number of students and faculty of color also find themselves feeling fragmented in this way in order to prove their intellectual worthiness. Learning to pass is thus about garnering a particular kind of respect within white academic spaces, and this is achieved at a profound cost to who you are.

What has led to the need for intellectual passing within the theological academy? The chief reason is that professional theological education in the United States was established in service to a white religious structure and order. Take my present context of Princeton Theological Seminary. Founded in 1812 by the Presbyterian denomination, the seminary was established to oversee the ministerial education of clergy—meaning white males. Prior to professional seminaries, clergy normally gained education through being tutored or apprenticed to an older, esteemed clergyperson. Such young men were prepared for ministry through shadowing other clergy leaders, working in their local parishes with them, and participating in the spiritual lives of the broader town. At the start of the nineteenth century, the Presbyterian church lamented that there was a shortage of young men being educated for clergy positions. Pulpits sat empty, without pastors to lead congregations. A few men within the Presbyterian church offered several proposals on how they might recruit and train generations of clergymen for ministry. One proposal was to establish a seminary at Princeton that followed the Andover model of professional theological training. Although there was conversation about establishing it as a divinity school of Princeton University or as a school that could compete with Princeton University by offering undergraduate classes, the Presbyterians decided to establish a separate graduate school for white men that focused on professional education for ministry.[2]

These young white clergymen were of a particular standing as well. Most came from white families who held land and property, benefiting in many ways from America's slave economy. In short, ministry as a profession was oriented toward young white men from wealthy backgrounds. Many of the men who attended Princeton Seminary early on were graduates of Harvard, Princeton University, and Yale, among other Ivy League colleges. This seminary envisioned producing white male clergy who not only led their respective parishes but also offered leadership in the social and political matters of a young nation, including social issues such as slavery. Clergymen were sought after to lead and ponder the nation's affairs. Princeton Theological Seminary was largely about producing "sound" ministers who could uphold and defend the Christian faith in an increasingly modern world, who could speak to the pressing social issues that threatened to tear apart the nation. The seminary had a highly classist and patriarchal understanding of who it was producing as leaders: white men of character and sound mind who would lead their communities and nation into God's truth. The early days of professional Protestant theological education were thus about the ministerial formation of educated men.[3]

Within white institutions like Princeton, when professional theological education was extended to people of color, it was in service to civilizing them. Professional theological education was not created with African Americans in mind, although "exceptional" African Americans would later gain entrance into white seminaries for the purposes of "cultural contact" in service to

Christianizing them (although it is important to note that African American seminaries were also emerging by 1867—a point to which I return in chapter 3). Princeton faculty saw their engagement with black persons as connected primarily to the project of civilizing and Christianizing racial others. Blacks who were enslaved represented the African heathen who were in need of saving from their pagan predilections. And black enslavement in America was inextricably tied to Protestant colonial impulses around the world.

In *Significations*, black religionist Charles Long talks about such Christianizing efforts and how they were described as "cultural exchange." Early on, those from the United States who engaged with other cultures presumed that they were participating in a model of cultural contact in efforts to bring true piety and progress to faraway worlds and to rid those worlds of practices and beliefs deemed to be heathenistic. The racist logic of cultural contact imposed upon people of color around the world was the same racist ideology that dehumanized Africans who were brought to the United States, leading to their enslavement.

Consider Archibald Alexander, first professor of Princeton Seminary, who delivered his inaugural address on August 12, 1812, extolling the beneficial effects of Christianity on other non-European nations based on an idea of cultural exchange. He stated:

> The beneficial effects of Christianity on those nations that have received it is a striking fact and furnishes a strong argument in favor of the authenticity and inspiration of the Scriptures. Under their benign influence, war has become less ferocious; justice has been more equally distributed; the poor have been more generally instructed; and their wants supplied; asylums have been provided for the unfortunate and distressed. The female character has been exalted to its proper standard in society . . . in short, the whole fabric of society has been meliorated; and real civilization promoted by Christianity wherever it has been received.[4]

41

Notice that one hears a narrative of innocence within this idea of cultural "exchange": America offered Christianity; non-Christian nations received it. The beneficial effects of civilization are grounded in relations of reciprocity between America and "others." The problem with this is that the realities of cultural expansion, of unjust appropriation of foreign lands, of African persons being ripped from their homelands and sold as human commodities in the transatlantic slave trade, of American Christianity being beaten into the enslaved by plantation owners and masters are ignored. All this violence is completely dismissed in the narrative of benign cultural contact. For America was not innocent. This nation engaged in cultural conquest. Cultural engagement between the United States and the rest of the world was built on *an entire economy of significations* at the heart of its colonial project.

Central to this racist, colonial project was the Christian religion. And this Christian racist project persisted in the United States as seen through black enslavement. White ministers saw this civilizing mission as highly beneficial to the enslaved within the United States, helping the enslaved actualize themselves as Christian citizens who could live into the ideal of Christian virtue. It was no secret that Alexander, alongside other Princeton faculty members such as Charles Hodge and Samuel Miller, owned slaves and felt some measure of paternalistic responsibility in bringing enslaved communities into spiritual and intellectual enlightenment.[5] Although some of these professors oscillated in their views of American slavery at times throughout their lives, they consistently believed that America could play a role in civilizing non-Europeans at home and abroad, whether through slavery or some other kind of segregated social arrangement.

To be honest about the beginnings of theological education, we must admit the racialization of professional theological education. Underrepresented, historically disadvantaged communities certainly recognize the ways in which theological education is tethered to a white power structure. Black students and faculty develop strategies to navigate this theological context successfully. One such strategy is intellectual passing, in which one accepts and integrates oneself into the work-reward structure of the academy, even when one feels harm and exhaustion from doing so. As a black woman, if I go along with the dominant categories, paradigms, and practices of my theological institution, I am much more likely to experience career mobility. This is a hard truth that even people of color hate to acknowledge.

Why would such a dubious practice tempt blacks? One reason is the hostility blacks encounter when they draw attention to the racist realities of the academy. For instance, I remember applying for a faculty position and being asked whether womanist theology was still a legitimate discourse. The questioner assumed that womanist theological studies had run its course, that it was a kind of identity politics that had been resolved through the civil rights movement and its assumed achievement of racial justice. So the interviewer was questioning why I would employ a perspective that she (presumably) perceived as irrelevant. I was baffled, first, because her assumption dismissed womanist theology as a legitimate mode of theological discourse altogether, and second, because her question placed the burden on me to prove the truth of ongoing intersectional experiences of structural racism out of which womanist theology grounds its modes of discourse. Through my response, I pushed back, but it came at a cost: when I was hired, I found myself participating in the emotionally draining work of being forced to engage this question over and over again with this senior colleague.

Why this clamor to prove or justify the truth of structural racism? Many theological institutions demand "evidence" or "data" of institutional racism within the theological academy. It is a demand that I find intellectually and institutionally dishonest. First, theological institutions and nationally governing bodies of theological education such as ATS have failed to document substantively the many experiences of structural racism that have occurred and continue to occur. Second, the question of empirical data or "evidence" in relation to the problem of race raises profound ethical issues for marginalized groups and often challenges the existence of racism itself. Consider the discourse surrounding public education. In America, teachers and policy experts are constantly bombarded with demands for "evidence" that young black children are disproportionately discriminated against in public education. Although numerous studies have corroborated gross discrimination on the basis of race in public education, institutional demands to prove the existence of structural racism persist.[6] These demands reinforce a particular assumption: that one must prove the existence of structural racism through the terms of elite white institutional power. Proof of racism is only legitimated through the institutional gaze.

Official segregation in the United States during the twentieth century is an important reminder of how white institutions and structures made impossible charges of structural racism. During Jim Crow, the judicial decision of the "separate but equal" clause created a problem of advocacy when speaking about segregation as a moral wrong, sin, or inequitable institution. Jim Crow was based on the premise that although the state sponsored a racially separate system, its separate institutions were equal in cultural, economic, social, educational, and political resources. Political leaders maintained that white and black communities had access to the same public education, employment, public facilities, restaurants, and more. In fact, political and religious leaders argued that Jim Crow was *moral* in the sense that it allowed communities to flourish unhindered by racial conflict and animosity. Southern states argued that segregation fostered equality between the "races," denying that segregation itself was racist and fostered an unequal system. The question of "evidence" remained central to the debate over the moral status of Jim Crow. Martin Luther King, James Baldwin, Ella Baker, and Septima Clark all spoke about the hypocrisy of white America, how it refused to acknowledge the racial pain and anger of black communities. Even today, the complaint that black shoppers are routinely followed through stores due to racist practices is met with the demand, "What *evidence* of that do you have?" This call for evidence in relation to racist institutional practice is grounded in the belief that white America is innocent. Given such an underlying belief of innocence, how can other people legitimate their claims of exploitation and injustice? How can they justify or "prove" that oppression exists?

This demand from white institutions to supply "evidence" is grounded in epistemic privilege, or how dominant groups are given authority and privilege in relation to the production and maintenance of particular forms of knowledge. For instance, in general the public does not consider sexism to be an empirical fact until both women *and men* confirm its existence. Dominant groups (in this case, of men) become the interpreters of these social realities, which points to the difficulties of "evidence"-based research on issues such as structural racism or patriarchy. I am not suggesting that scholarship oriented toward data on injustices is unnecessary or simply a capitulation to the status quo. Rather, I am raising a question about *the limits* of evidence and how structures often disallow particular voices from contributing to the "data" related to injustices. Take Michelle Alexander's groundbreaking book *The New Jim Crow*. Her text draws upon critical race scholarship and offers diverse data on the structural racism that grounds and colors the criminal justice system. The genius of her work is that she uses "evidence"-based research to demonstrate the new ways in which structural racism exists, in this case in our thoroughly racist criminal justice system.

Yet the fastest-growing group of persons who are unjustly targeted by the criminal justice system is black and brown women. This fact is completely absent in Alexander's groundbreaking work. It matters that she offers a compelling case for the existence of this new Jim Crow that has had a disproportionate effect on black men. However, the narratives of black and brown women remain underarticulated, even silenced. Alexander does not give any attention to gender in relation to structural racism and the criminal justice system. On the one hand, Alexander's analysis shows us that we need *better* evidence in order to see how mass incarceration affects all marginalized groups. On the other hand, focusing on this example shows the limits of evidence itself, as it never quite captures the fullness of the claims we make about certain realities. What might these incarcerated women (or other marginalized groups like incarcerated sexual minorities) speak about that may not be totally grasped in empirical and evidential-based models? While evidence-based approaches can be profoundly helpful, we would do well to practice greater moderation in our total dependence on and demand for evidence-based models. These models can fail. So while elite institutional contexts often demand evidence, evidence has its *limits*, as evidence often fails to capture other experiences and modes of knowledge. In other words, calls for evidence are never neutral. A politics is always involved.

This demand for evidence is present in the theological academy, even though the academy's history is marked by clear institutional disenfranchisement of people of color. People demand evidence for institutional whiteness. Yet how can we develop substantial, evidence-based studies of how race (gender and class as well) plays a role in hiring, salary compensation, and tenure when there is little or no policy in academic institutions that requires the transparency of such processes? Consider the opaque process that many women of color endure in the theological academy. A number of black women theological scholars employ womanist and black feminist perspectives. They are told that the process of tenure review involves having one major academic book published (that is not your dissertation), a book that makes a significant intervention in and contribution to the field. However, their intellectual work is often perceived as less rigorous than that of white scholars. And the perceived rigor of any particular discourse, they are told, directly affects its "legibility."

Legibility (or legitimacy) of writing is central to tenure, but this idea of legibility functions in hegemonic ways. If one does not frame womanist theological arguments from an analytical standpoint (and in conversation with major white philosophical and theological traditions), senior scholars (and hence, university tenure committees as well) assume that such arguments are not adding to the field. Moreover, womanist theological discourse is grounded in part in narrative epistemology that may resist (although not always) linear forms of argumentation as the only way to construct a valid perspective, troubling the logic of a closed philosophical system. In part, narrative epistemology is about rethinking the limits of abstract modes of theorization, opting to ask how practice tames the kind of theoretical claims we can make. For instance, some womanist scholars find themselves wanting to talk about Christology from the viewpoint of critical social theory or ethnographic approaches rather than strictly doctrinal debates. However, this is often not a legible or legitimate move for scholars, as Christology belongs to the doctrinal domain of theological thought. As a result, this idea of legibility ends up reading black woman scholars as nonrigorous, nonsubstantive, and unwilling to engage the (white) "tradition." This is an example of how whiteness then structures and determines the tenure review process for many black women.

Studies in theological education have not really mapped this double bind of racism and hetero-patriarchy that women of color face in the theological academy. As a result, black women scholars such as Stephanie Buckhanon Crowder find themselves fighting for their perspectives to be seen as true and legitimate within the broader academy. In Crowder's case, she writes that as the first African American woman in her department, at the end of every semester for five years she was summoned to the "principal's office." She states: "A parent's phone call, a student's email, an evaluation or comment, and there I was waiting to hear the charges and my subsequent punishment."[7] Institutional administrators such as deans and faculty committees often tell black women scholars such as Crowder that their perspectives exaggerate claims of racism or don't properly capture other aspects that could have led to tenure denial. In short, those in power treat these women with contempt and regard their perspectives as misguided and inaccurate depictions of the academic context.

47

As a result, these women find themselves caught in an unending cycle of frustration, as some power brokers view as illegitimate their interpretations of their own academic situation.

* * *

Learning to pass requires acquiescing intellectually to a static conception of the knowledge formation process. An example: As a student at Yale in 2002, I encountered what were typically presented as two categories of theological thought: classical and contextual. While I will dispute the categories, I will retain the prevailing names here for clarity. This divinity school treated classical theological thought as a form of knowledge that is prior to experience, a kind of universal description of human social and religious realities. Thus some professors at Yale did not give sufficient treatment to how classical theological concepts associated with Calvin or Barth are historically constituted and shaped in and through the cultural processes of their own time (and therefore as contingent as discourses produced by Cone or Cannon). I often heard white students ask how a black theological thinker such as Cone could possibly be related to their (white) theological journey when a teacher placed such a thinker on the syllabus. But those same white students simply assumed that Barth was relevant to students across racial and denominational affiliations. This made it awkward and even unintelligible/illegitimate (to the white majority) to ask whether Barth was relevant to or desirable for, say, a black theological journey. Similarly, because that school interpreted Barth's or Calvin's theology as the definitive discourse on Christian doctrine, it automatically tamed or dismissed any cultural inadequacies or limitations associated with such discourses. Through such processes, classical modes of theological knowledge become upheld as universal and its categories become the interpretive grid through which all other forms of religious experience are evaluated.

Within some classical modes, theological epistemology takes on a kind of rigid, unyielding, absolutist quality. Any *other* mode of knowing is discounted as wrong. As a result, the knowledge formation process was an "either/or" epistemological structure, a zero-sum game within a religiously pluralistic context. Institutional contexts that privilege classical modes of theological thought are often unable to acknowledge and wrestle with the cultural conditioning and contingencies of classical discourses. Because these scholars treat classical thought as the universal standard, this attitude often automatically excludes different ways of knowing ourselves and God's action within the worlds we inhabit.

Yet many faculty and students resist privileging these classical modes, posing such questions as: Should the foundations of theological reflection (theological categories) be treated as something that can be accessed prior to experience? Can predetermined theological categories provide meanings for lived experience, or do lived experiences help us rethink the meanings of those very categories? Or both? Introductory classes to theology or theological ethics typically spend significant time on predetermined categories in explaining the meanings of Christian faith. Presenting historical categories is not a problem in itself. The problem is that these categories are interpreted as the *only* ones, or are *taught* in a way that disallows other voices, themes, and projects. People of color (and even many white students) often encounter these categories as discourses alien to their own social locations. The predetermined meanings simply do not match their lived experiences. Students find themselves in a bind, at war with theologies that attempt to dictate the meanings of their own Christian faith. This dominant model of theological education is thus about mastery and production of a "pure" knowledge, a knowledge untouched by the contradictions and diversity of human experience itself.

This has led in the last several decades to the emergence of subaltern theological and religious voices who have challenged univocal modes of knowing marked by classical white theology. These subaltern perspectives highlight narrative modes of knowing, which gesture toward the plurality of theological knowledge, expanding what we say about God, humans, and the world. While the theological academy is steadily embracing these subaltern discourses, these modes of theological discourse are cited as "contextual," meaning other, not mainstream, as if white/dominant perspectives aren't also contextual.

Describing these theologies as contextual comes at a profound price. As a professor of color, I often lament with other faculty of color how contextual courses are treated within the institutional life of a school. Within the curricula, contextual courses are often not "required," while classical courses are. This hierarchy of classical and contextual courses has tremendous implications for faculty of color, especially those who are pretenured. When a pretenured faculty member teaches a set of courses that are not required, it affects how this faculty member is assessed during the tenure-review process. Moreover, students are able to matriculate through an entire program without taking a single course on issues of difference by a black professor or another professor of color. I often wonder what is lost when white students preparing for ministry are not required to take courses that help them wrestle with the browning of Christianity in this nation and around the globe—even in their own future congregations.

Nevertheless, schools rigorously defend classical modes as essential *because they are historical sources.* Scholars argue that these historical sources are necessary to understand the orthodoxy of Christian faith itself. And orthodoxy is tied to western European, white theologians and theorists. In my estimation, most of these courses begin with white male theological thinkers whom the (largely male and white) institutions understand to be the shapers of the discourse. I teach a course entitled "Theories of Justice: A Decolonial Investigation." When students arrive in the class, I watch their faces register surprise at the fact that we will be reading postcolonial, feminist, and other subaltern voices *first*. These voices supply the class with central interpretive categories on ideas of justice that will then function as the central framework from which they reread "classical" philosophical and theological texts on justice. What would it mean to reread Rawls, Habermas, Niebuhr, Rauschenbusch, and others through the decolonial categories that alternative theologians and theorists provide, theologians and theorists who have different intellectual starting points? Students immediately notice that the major questions about justice may shift and change when using this approach. They begin to understand that one's perspectives and beliefs depend on one's positionality or situatedness, that one often cannot see the perspectives and beliefs that are furthest from one's own.

The dominant theological inquiries of white men typically set the intellectual priorities of theological discourse, a discourse that then almost inevitably evaluates other inquiries outside of their norm as peripheral, contingent, contextual, and particular (as opposed to the assumed "universal reach" of classical theological ideas and questions). For example, within the history of theology and ethics, the question of "the virtues" has dominated how theology has thought historically about moral action and moral reasoning. In the past, discourses on the virtues have primarily focused on individual character formation within community with less robust analyses of *what counts* as virtue as well as the limits of exercising virtues within asymmetrical relations of power. This institutional analysis of the virtues and how to account for power in relation to virtue has been central to African American theological critiques of the European virtue tradition. Epistemologically, virtue cannot be understood outside of social processes and institutional structures of power that disenfranchise. (Aristotle, the source of so much thinking about the virtues, acknowledged this frankly, explicitly embedding his theory of virtue in an account that justified slavery.) Notice how this way of talking about virtue outside of social matrices obscures what is at stake for marginalized communities. Consequently, many scholars of color have not engaged this tradition significantly, as this tradition creates anxieties about its ability to foster human flourishing for vulnerable populations.

Because the educational aim is mastery of classical knowledge rooted in white thinkers, the seminary or divinity school often leaves unaddressed how students cultivate themselves as moral agents in a *diverse* world. Mastering technical knowledge becomes the end of theological education. How to interpret Barth, Hegel, or Schleiermacher becomes the goal. Mastery of classroom knowledge is primary. In order to pass intellectually, native sons and daughters accept this reality and perform intellectual mastery to experience the rewards associated with climbing the career ladder. Focusing on the capacities students need to transform the worlds they inhabit is secondary within so many conventional white seminaries and divinity schools. As a result, they ignore or give less attention to vocational skills like antiracist or antisexist leadership in social spaces.

To give an example: Many seminaries and divinity schools around the nation (particularly elite or prestigious schools) are debating whether to require a class devoted specifically to forms of structural racism. Such debate tends to obscure the more important point: that a required course (or required courses) on racism signals that the institution is committed to shaping seminary students who can respond to the profound racial anxiety, fear, and violence that pervade society. In an increasingly hostile racial environment in which white supremacist groups are articulating their racist views overtly, seminaries and divinity schools recognize the importance of establishing and approving a course (or courses) that all students are required to take in order to develop habits and skills in the area of antiracist struggle. We witness pastors who are often paralyzed and unsure what to say to their congregations or communities about the current racial antagonisms and violence. Confused, many pastors mute themselves, choosing to say nothing about the critical racial moment we are experiencing. This surely is a failure of leadership. It is also a failure of education.

This move to include race/ethnicity as a curriculum requirement has been controversial. Typically, it raises questions about who will teach a required race course. Will this course further burden people of color who often bear the brunt of teaching and "educating" seminary and church communities on racial justice? What kind of role do white professors play in educating the student body about questions of racial in/justice? These are fair questions that point to the distribution of work in any seminary's commitment to teaching antiracist praxis. Black and brown professors cannot be solely responsible for this antiracist education; it must be the responsibility of the entire community.

Instead of one required course on race, some schools are opting to offer a few courses in each department that explore questions of racial in/justice. Princeton Theological Seminary has embraced this model. However, this departmental requirement forces some professors to teach material with which they are unfamiliar, undermining their sense of academic freedom (although one could question why teaching unfamiliar material would be a problem if scholars imagine the intellectual life as one of curiosity and ever-expanding growth). These questions of academic freedom when teaching are part of an ongoing conversation and are perhaps a legitimate concern. Yet, how can students wrestle with matters of race/ethnicity if professors (that is, teachers) are unwilling to wrestle with how race shapes their own discipline and broader view of theological education?

Requiring courses in race/ethnicity demonstrates that race and racism are *theological* issues. Racism is *sin*. Identifying racism in this way helps institutions of theological education rethink how a race/ethnicity requirement produces a particular kind of agent and leader that we want within churches and broader social and political spaces. *What good is it to produce leaders for churches, social movements, and other faith communities who can interpret Barth or Tillich but cannot interpret their communities that are plagued by racial anger, frustration, and vio-*

lence? Theological education must take seriously the process of forming subjects, which means considering questions of race as central to what it means to articulate a gospel of love and justice. Students must see their vocation inextricably linked to how they embody justice and flourishing as they engage with other ethnic/racial communities. How students embody leadership in relation to racial justice is key, and this means that technical knowledge in the classroom cannot be the singular interest and goal of theological education.

Learning to pass means acquiescing to, even accepting, this entire state of affairs in theological education. As a native daughter, I often felt that I had to embrace this traditional model of mastery in order to prove my intellectual worthiness. I must demonstrate mastery of these traditional forms of knowledge and ways of knowing on top of my own area of specialization. Learning to pass often requires either repressing or compartmentalizing more dynamic forms of learning that do not neatly align with what is already the proven intellectual system. I have often experienced deep frustration and even anger as a native daughter who certainly finds joy in all kinds of knowledge and learning yet does not want to be beholden to the privileged, dominant way of knowing that pervades and marks many institutions of theological education.

* * *

The question lingers whether the theological academy can be "home" for racial-ethnic minority students and faculty around the nation. It has been home for me, a site of partial welcoming and flourishing, but not without deep frustrations and problems. In the academic context, many historically marginalized groups such as African Americans, Asian Americans, and Latinx Americans constantly endure the tension of being an insider/outsider. Black students are not the only students of color who experience double consciousness. Over the last few years, I have learned more about the racial frustrations and pain of Asian

Americans in theological institutions. Many tenure-track Asian scholars have expressed to me the angst associated with intellectual passing. One good friend discussed with me what so many young Asian Americans focus on in their doctoral work: to prove themselves within the white-dominant work-reward structure by choosing to focus on a classical white figure or discourse. At times, this is the true desire of Asian doctoral students. At other times, they are interested in exploring Asian American topics but are instructed to explore those themes once they are tenured. To be fair, this advice seems strategic, as there are few positions in Asian American studies or Asian American theology. However, this advice also shows the narrow perspective of the theological guild itself, which compels some Asian American scholars to repress or ignore what drives and informs their theological work and vocational aspirations. Some do want to reset or contribute to the theological enterprise through this more specific work. Yet fear persists, as this work will either pigeonhole them or make them less competitive in the market. Theological institutions have not yet expanded themselves enough to hire, for example, an Asian American scholar for a systematic theology position who has done a dissertation on an Asian American figure or school of thought. Search committees often default to someone whose dissertation is on Barth, Calvin, Aquinas, or another "grounding" classical (meaning white) figure. In addition, the religious and cultural differences of Asian American students are left unaddressed altogether, leaving them feeling uncared for and ignored. These kinds of experiences let me know that the insider/outsider is experienced even in this community, although in qualitatively different ways from black students.

Over the last several years, there has been an explosion of protests within universities and within the theological academy among black students and faculty. These protests among students have certainly coincided with larger dissenting campaigns related to racial profiling, police killings, and other acts of racial aggression in our country. Many students experience academic contexts as unsafe spaces in which to lament the injustices that people of color face daily. Moreover, such students feel they are unable to lament the macro and micro racial aggressions (such as passing) they experience in the seminary or divinity school. Faculty and students of color describe the psychological assault and trauma they endure, from the classrooms to the dorm rooms. For these faculty and students, the theological academy feels like both a home and a nightmare.

For instance, in 2017 we witnessed a national debate on the problem of structural racism at Duke Divinity School. The *New York Times* published an article on May 9, 2017, chronicling the fight that ensued between Paul Griffiths, a professor of Catholic theology, and a number of faculty of color (and women) over a diversity-training session that was to happen at Duke Divinity School. Duke faculty member Anathea Portier-Young emailed her colleagues about a two-day session aimed at combating racism in which she stated that this diversity program was "transformative, powerful, and life-changing." Griffiths disagreed. In an email reply, he urged his colleagues not to attend or "waste their time." He described this diversity program as possessing "illiberal roots" and "totalitarian tendencies." The response of the dean included publicly reprimanding Griffiths over a faculty email list for what seemed to be his facilitation of a hostile work environment toward people of color and women. The dean noted that it was inappropriate and unacceptable to use mass email to contest programs that directly address institutional racism, sexism, or any other form of disenfranchisement. The debate, which became national news, ended with Griffiths resigning, taking early retirement.

What is particularly interesting is how the *New York Times* framed the debate. The headline of the article read "A New Battleground over Political Correctness."[8] By terming this debate a problem of political correctness, the *New York Times* gestured toward the legitimacy of Griffiths's viewpoint, even granting primacy to his stance. If this were an issue of political correctness, one would presume that Griffiths was being attacked and backed into a corner, forced to be politically correct, stripped of his right to exercise free speech. In this interpretation, Griffiths is the victim, the actor who is being assaulted within an autocratic academic system. But is this really what was going on? This interpretation recalls the general cries of many white individuals, inside and outside the academy, who feel that they are experiencing "reverse racism" or psychological assault whenever they are invited or required to engage substantively with racial history and current practices in this country. These white groups reduce quests for racial justice to mere problems of political correctness.

Indeed, interpreting the Duke case as a problem of political correctness obscures what may be at stake. The *New York Times*'s framing of this incident at Duke completely dismisses or ignores the historical context out of which these kinds of debates occur. Within university settings, diversity and antiracist programs were established to combat the historical and contemporary institutional disenfranchisement that people of color experience. As of 2016, a new study from the Teachers Insurance and Annuity Association (TIAA) Institute demonstrated that although US colleges and universities have increased faculty diversity, most gains have *not* been tenure track or tenured. This is a complex story. Ironically, just as the doors of academe have opened up more and more to underrepresented and marginalized groups over the last few decades, the available jobs tend not to be the conventionally "good" jobs, which come with higher salaries, better benefits, and especially the possibility of tenure.[9] On the one hand, women have experienced the largest growth trajectory as faculty in the academy, nearly doubling their numbers, especially in two-year colleges. Even some ethnic minorities like Asian Americans have experienced a major increase in faculty representation, especially in research universities. African American faculty numbers have shot up, signaling greater access to teaching jobs among this group. Yet women faculty continue to be less likely to hold full-time appointments and even less likely to ever break through the ranks to full professorship (9 percent have achieved it, up slightly from 6 percent in 1993). More ethnic minoritized faculty have landed tenure over the last few decades, but so many others have not or have been actively denied this academic prize. For certain, this shrinkage of good jobs has affected groups across racial, ethnic, and gender affiliations.

However, the reason for the relatively stagnant progress among women and African Americans, for example, is due to other "core value" factors in the academy that reflect racial and gender bias in the hiring and promotion process. For example, determining what constitutes rigorous scholarship to receive tenure or what qualifies a scholar to receive full professorship is made by white institutional structures that privilege models of classical scholarship I have discussed already, models that marginalized scholars often find themselves needing to fit into or "pass" in order to be legible and therefore worthy.

Scholars of color are often told that they are not "theoretical enough" or are illegible/illegitimate within the field because they are working from different scholarly paradigms and frameworks that are not decidedly Eurocentric. In many research universities and nonresearch colleges, it is primarily white male scholars who make these decisions. This creates an academic context that is rife with racial and gender bias, which disproportionately hinders scholars of color from surviving in minimal ways (such as getting an academic job that allows them to stay above the poverty level).

It is this historical and current problem related to racial injustice in the academy that precipitated the kinds of diversity programs Portier-Young of Duke commended. These programs are not just another ideological stance. They are grounded in historical and current privations and injustices that people of color endure. They cannot be interpreted simply as another instantiation of political correctness.

Thankfully, some journalists understood the structural problems associated with the Duke debacle. Black students at Duke Divinity School labeled the racial milieu at Duke a "nightmare." In an NPR article, Nick Chiles documented the responses of black ministry students at Duke in relation to the debate. Ironically, black students felt they were constantly targeted by white faculty and students for speaking out on the antiblack animus within the academic community and larger society. One black student recounted hearing a white classmate calling a black classmate "ghetto." Another student remembers a white classmate calling a black classmate a "jigaboo," although the white student claimed to not understand the meaning of the term. Most troubling was an incident in which a white student confronted a black student in a most inhumane way, using the word "nigger."[10] These incidents attempted to situate the Griffiths debate within the larger cultural ethos at Duke Divinity School that appears to be hostile to students of color. They make it clear that there are larger issues at stake here than "political correctness."

In his article, Chiles highlights the testimony of one former Duke Divinity School student, Carl Kenny, who adds another layer of information to the racial hostility many black students experienced at Duke by connecting this kind of issue to white economic and ecclesial interests. Kenny argues that Duke Divinity has become increasingly inhospitable to students and faculty of color (and their viewpoints on the persistence of racism) due to the influence of a conservative white evangelical community inside the United Methodist Church. Funding of seminaries such as Duke comes from conservative evangelical entities who do not see racism as something to be addressed within theological education or broader society. Many white scholars discourage black students that stand in liberation traditions because such scholars do not see liberationist racial analyses as fair examinations of what has gone wrong with theological education and American churches (some white scholars feel these discourses exaggerate or overstate their claims). I have personally witnessed white colleagues label such students "emotional," "subjective," uncritical, and trying to be "politically correct."[11]

The voices of marginalized students revive what is at stake in the Duke debate. However, Duke Divinity School is not alone. Many seminaries and divinity schools share this problem. While on sabbatical in 2016, I was a visiting professor at Yale University Divinity School and witnessed protests over the issue of structural racism. While some schools have since fought to address these concerns, others have simply maintained the conservative line, contributing to the pain and trauma of students and faculty of color within theological education.

This NPR article demonstrates the limitations of the *New York Times* reporting on this issue. In large part, it demonstrates that society often does not consider the questions, concerns, or grievances of racial-ethnic communities. I find myself incredibly grieved by the potential claim that my tenure, for example, demonstrates that white supremacy is losing its foothold in spaces of higher education. I think not. Despite my personal victory of receiving tenure, the numbers of minoritized faculty in ATS schools are shamefully flat, especially given the increased diversity in the student population. Even with tenured cases like mine, white supremacy still operates through standards of tenure and promotion in theological education as well as through other formalized markers of respect and authority, whether that is governance committees at universities, guilds, or in the shaping of curricula. Yet, when I was learning to pass, I was often careful how I raised these overt problems of white supremacy, being sure to defer to white standards and norms of institutional authority even as I disagreed. Learning to pass is not just about desiring the benefits (academic respect, tenure security, benefits such health-care insurance, etc.) of white institutional spaces but about attempting to survive and thrive when you know these spaces are detrimental to your own sense of authenticity and vocational health.

White supremacy in spaces of higher education (like the theological academy) has morphed over time. Leaders in theological education proclaim that they have hired more women and ethnic minorities than in the past. They see this as evidence that racism is reversing in our spaces. It is not. Even if a historically white school makes progress in hiring scholars of color, this is not the end of structural racism. There are entire white cultural codes, norms, and standards that still shape and structure the benefit-reward system in theological education such as tenure, promotion, guild benefits, and more. The theological academy must begin to pay serious attention to its native daughters and sons of racial-ethnic groups who possess profound wisdom about what is wrong with theological education. Theological education is home for many of us, but we equally find ourselves being treated as strangers through these experiences of structural racism. The way forward involves acknowledging the past in order to deal with institutional bigotry in the present.

* * *

While the academy is oftentimes a limiting context, theological education is indeed home for me. I have experienced tremendous possibilities in the academic context, possibilities that might be described as complex and tentative rather than absolute. Consider why many people enroll in divinity school or seminary in the first place. Many students enter theological educational contexts because they are *angry* with the church. Students often come expressing that they are fighting with their church communities over urgent issues that relate directly to their identity and sense of call. They feel their churches are rigid, unbending, and irrelevant. These young people come to seminary believing or hoping that the theological academy will be a safe space to ask questions they often cannot ask in their own traditions. I remember that when I arrived at Yale Divinity School, I found myself asking many questions that would not have been acceptable to ask in my Pentecostal tradition. I reclaimed the questions I had at nine years of age surrounding gender and class disparities in black churches. I also began to ask new questions, interrogating my own theological views in relation to LGBTQ and interreligious issues. I found myself wading in new waters. But I also had new tools to keep me afloat in seminary through my engagement with a plethora of thinkers, texts, and conversational partners from a diversity of ecclesial and cultural backgrounds. I wanted to swim out into the deep, albeit with aids that could keep me above water.

CHAPTER 2

The theological academy as both a limiting experience and a reservoir of possibilities has created a paradoxical existence for me, one of existential and intellectual quandaries. The academic site at which I was intellectually shaped was both liberating and deeply oppressive. It was a context that affirmed thinking critically about my inherited ideas and future theological strivings while at the same time suppressing and devaluing *the very cultural experiences that allowed me to think theologically in the first place*. I felt paralyzed.

This reality captures the dilemma that many students experience, especially students of color. Having been a theological professor for almost a decade, I am well aware that many black students share this testimony. They arrive with high expectations, trusting that seminaries will model inclusive and compassionate community. They hope that their cultural and religious experiences, although different from the Euro-American norm, will be respected and integrated into institutional practices and the overall learning environment. Instead, many of them experience a full-out intellectual and existential assault, even as they may also experience the academic context as somewhat liberating (giving them space to think critically and to grow intellectually and spiritually). They are told that their experiences are "cultural," not theological. Their respective religious traditions are treated in peripheral ways, seen as hostile or irrelevant to theological education altogether. Moreover, black students are constantly underestimated and told (in multiple ways) that they are less rigorous and intellectually serious than their white counterparts. These students often report that their academic experiences paradoxically feel liberating yet profoundly frustrating. These students want to know how they can pursue intellectual acumen and spiritual formation in a way that does not dishonor who they are culturally, a way that instead makes room for critical yet generous critique. These students want to pursue their vocation in a way that allows them to bring their entire self to the intellectual and theological enterprise. But the academy often disallows that. It disallows intellectual authenticity. As a result,

62

such students discover one thing: they must adapt to the dominant environment (learn to pass) in ways that leave behind (or compartmentalize) their own cultural languages and religious vocabularies.

Black students who have a *precarious* relationship with their white mentors typically feel such intellectual passing most acutely. Consider this hypothetical scenario of a doctoral student I will refer to as Connie, a scenario that is often the narrative of black students. Connie is an African American woman PhD student at an elite university. Having Baptist and Pentecostal roots, she studies constructive theology with a focus on notions of Christology in relation to racial and gender justice. She is interested in engaging christological ideas with womanist and postcolonial theological discourses. In part, she locates herself between historical and contemporary theological discourses in a way that demonstrates creative tension. However, within the larger academy, there is often this expectation that one will "take sides" intellectually: one is either Calvinist *or* postcolonial, Barthian *or* womanist, Hauerwasian *or* liberationist. These strict binaries make room for only one kind of theological identity, forcing doctoral students to check which box they fit. Connie certainly feels this pressure to conform to the binary categories that provide theological identity. She needs to pass by choosing a category that can capture her intellectual identity.

Yet Connie is painfully aware that these binaries are associated with the white intellectual environment of the academy in which she is situated. She knows she participates in scholarly discourses that have been shaped by white intellectuals from the start. Connie therefore must take a side: Will she be a theologically liberal or conservative voice? For theological liberalism or against theological liberalism? The frustration, in this case, is that Connie can only position herself and come to visibility and voice through these predetermined binary categories. She can only be made legible and legitimate in and through two primary theological identities—liberal or conservative, through Cone or Barth, through Williams or Ruether. Connie can only find her voice as an *echo*. In short, the theological educational system is set up so that many ethnic/racialized students can experience their voices only as a distant replica of the binary theological identities already available within the scholarly discourse. Discouraged from *creatively thinking themselves into* new theological spaces, students like Connie find themselves in a bind. The system disempowers them from asking what new kinds of theological identities are yet to be imagined in relation to their theological interests and commitments.

This bind creates a precarious situation between PhD students of color and their white mentors. On the one hand, these relationships are marked by gratitude, as doctoral students from underrepresented communities are given a chance to learn their area of study from well-respected, top scholars in the field. The mentors are often personally invested in seeing these doctoral students succeed and contribute to the field in new ways. The doctoral students feel at ease approaching the field with their unique intellectual inquiries. On the other hand, such students feel the ambivalence that their mentors often express. This ambivalence is about seeing particular ethnic scholarly interests as too "narrow" or "lacking evidence." Certain marginalized discourses that critique canonical ideas in the field can even be seen as "hostile." These PhD students might find themselves offering a defense of their chosen methodological and topical path of study.

This ambivalence expressed by white mentors is not always overt. At times, white mentors might not even be aware that they possess and communicate this ambivalence to students. It is an ambivalence that can be expressed in covert ways—such as asking doctoral students to make sure their contemporary leanings are grounded in the concerns or questions of canonical thinkers (instead of being in conversation with such thinkers, demonstrating the equal grounding that both schools of thought stand on). And in this case students find themselves facing an academic ultimatum: either they conform their intellectual interests and research to the canonical ideas approved by the mentor, or they leave the program in hopes of landing in another program that can support their interests. They are faced with the dilemma of intellectual passing. This is a very difficult conversation, as doctoral students feel that these relationships are profoundly encouraging *and* limiting.

This bind is also readily apparent when master's students come to seminary, study with radical white and black mentors, and then are called to go back into their religious communities to lead. They go back to their communities with typically one of two theological visions—liberal or conservative. But neither vision may work for their contexts. There, they attempt to translate their academic theological learning within their "home" church spaces, only to be met with confusion or disinterest. This becomes a major source of frustration to seminarians who feel they have paid their dues by studying at a reputable seminary/divinity school in order to be effective. Yet, effectiveness is typically linked to mastering a body of knowledge, writing papers flawlessly, and being open to other views. Certainly, these are important skills and capacities to cultivate. However, something more is needed within their native communities. And these students often realize (even while progressing through the master's program) that the quality of relationships they have with their professors is both instructive *and* unhelpful. The student-mentor relationship and the classes themselves do not even consider ways of thinking and engaging their communities, although their relationships with such professors have often pushed students in challenging and rewarding directions. These students need to think through other theological frameworks beyond the binary categories that will help them fashion alternative theological spaces. Students of color are left asking: How do I create another kind of theological space? This question is not merely a fashionable endeavor, for this new kind of theological space is *required* within the very communities they serve. Their theological approaches are bound up with issues of survival against structural and psychic forms of racial bias.

This brief discussion on the precarious relationships that

black students have with their white mentors and their theological leanings reflects the larger problem I noted early in this chapter: the problem of whiteness. Institutional whiteness continues to drive the meanings, aims, and ends of theological education. Unfortunately, institutional whiteness plays out in the shape of professor/student relationships and affects spaces outside the academy as students return to their communities, where many of them are leaders.

These precarious relationships also disclose how black students often have to invest in institutional whiteness. Investment in institutional whiteness might simply amount to adopting a scholarly identity based on normative (white) terms of the field, reflecting a desire to pass. Doctoral students from underrepresented communities find themselves wanting or needing to "play the game." Yet, playing the academic game is less about blind ambition and more about survival. For PhD students, to produce an intellectual project that is somehow contrary to the existing canonical scholarship is to be considered less than a bona fide scholar and thus to be less competitive and desirable on the job market.

I think here of Monica Coleman's seminal essay, "Must I Be a Womanist?"[12] In part, this essay attempts to address the problem of how scholars of color (in the case of Coleman's article, black women scholars) must identify within structures of whiteness in order to be legible. While scholars rightly debated Coleman's diagnosis of the theological and political content of womanism, I am interested in what else her essay tracks, namely, how the identity marker "womanist" becomes a form of scholarly legibility and legitimacy in service to theologically liberal academic structures of whiteness. In this case, identifying as a womanist scholar serves market forces within many theological institutions. For example, over the last several decades, institutions in theological education have included womanist courses in their curricula. More seminaries have attempted to offer courses in "diversity" and contextual theologies, courses that count toward degrees in divinity schools and seminaries. On the one hand, this is a worthy achievement, as womanist scholarship continues to be marginalized within institutions in other kinds of ways (for example, when assessing tenure and promotion cases among black women scholars). Although womanist scholarship bears the brunt of continued ostracism, Coleman raises questions about the institutionalization of womanist scholarship in other ways (such as curriculum) and how such institutionalization bars other forms of black scholarly identity from entering into institutional commitments and demands.

What happens when a black woman does not identify as womanist and her research or teaching is not directly related to womanist scholarship? How is she rendered legible in the academic market that has particular assumptions about what black women scholars should be producing and bringing to the school? Coleman raises an important point about when scholarly identity markers like "womanist" reinforce certain investments of whiteness within the academy. The ability to "place" a black woman scholar in a "category" that offers coherence within broader liberal discourses on theological and racial diversity reflects problems of structural whiteness. The problem with this institutional investment in "false diversity" is that these institutions lose their critical edge on what it means to divest from institutional whiteness. All white administrators need to do is have a womanist scholar on staff along with the courses she teaches on this topic. The paradox is that even when a womanist refuses the terms of whiteness, the market forces of institutional whiteness can capitalize on womanist identity in ways that serve the academic status quo. This complicates how scholars of color such as black women navigate and negotiate white academic contexts they nevertheless call home.

* * *

How does one resist the desire to pass? I am struck by the life and legacy of the late Dr. James Cone. While attending a memorial service for him at Riverside Church in New York City in 2018,

I realized that his entire academic and activist life was a refusal to be seduced by the temptation to pass. In large part, his desire was about giving voice to black communities out of which he was born and claimed his identity. His goal was unapologetically to offer a counternarrative to dominant narratives of white supremacy that attempted to thwart and destroy black life. Growing up in Bearden, Arkansas, during segregation, Cone insisted that only truth telling could bring justice and healing to racial divisions in this country and around the world. He was fierce and unbending in his purpose. And it colored how he oriented his teaching and scholarship: toward justice.

Cone did not desire to pass intellectually because it was clear that he wanted to keep his work accountable to the material forms of black life he actually knew and defended. For example, Cone doesn't theorize black theology from some abstract place. He roots his idea of black theology in the black power movement that some black Christian clergy were embracing in the 1960s as seen through the *Black Manifesto*. He constructs a black theology out of the existential questions a number of black Christians faced under duress of white supremacist Christianity: Could one be "black" and Christian? For Cone, the answer to this question had to be deeply connected to the longings, yearning, fears, and dreams of black people. As a result, his aim in being a scholar was less about climbing the career ladder or being seen as "rigorous" and more about making clear the truth of white Christian assault on black life. It was only through exposing Christian assault on black communities that Cone could render theologically sound the need for black liberation.

Cone's desire to stay accountable to black life and its diverse material forms meant that he did not live the life of a secluded scholar. Part of the game of intellectually passing requires scholars of color isolating themselves to buy into academic ideas of prowess that involve individual competition among scholars. If one wants to receive particular funding for excellent research at one's university, one is required to "distinguish oneself" from (compete with) one's academic colleagues. This often becomes a treacherous game that destroys any possibility of intellectual col-laboration and collective creativity. Cone refused this academic game and even called it out as part of structural racism.

Most important, Cone's refusal to pass is also seen in where he locates himself: within a revolutionary community of schol-ars. Throughout his life, he was always seen in deep community and conversation with other academics who were giving voice to black life, academics such as Gayraud Wilmore, J. Deotis Roberts, Katie Cannon, Jacquelyn Grant, Cornel West, and oth-ers. These scholars might be understood as a "collective" who gained tremendous strength in creating an alternate scholarly context out of which their work could gain life and flourish. I would like to think that this community of scholars sustained the work of Cone and countless others who imagined their schol-arship being in service to decolonizing and freeing people's minds, hearts, and bodies from racist, hetero-patriarchal, and classist oppression.

I am not suggesting that Cone was perfect. After all, much debate among his own students revolves around his lack of us-ing black sources as well as his absence in naming problems of gender and sexual justice in his early theological work. However, what made Cone deeply successful was that he *did not abandon the black cultural languages and religious vocabularies out of which he was raised.* This took me a while to learn as a Pentecostal. And it is a lesson with which other scholars of color must wrestle.

I do acknowledge that there are profound costs and risks when one chooses to resist the reward-producing structures of the academy in order to exercise integrity in one's own intellec-tual life. The risk is always there. But Cone took it. And he didn't take this leap of faith alone: he took it with other revolutionary thinkers within the academy and in the larger world who were committed to a different kind of reward. But being willing to take the risk means rethinking one's notion of success, for not everyone who takes risks like Cone ends up as a full professor at a place like Union Theological Seminary. Some are locked out of academic structures altogether. I am aware of my own success despite various risks I have taken as well, risks that other close friends have taken, only to be met with institutional violence. So, there are no perfect answers. But Cone sheds light on the dilemma of passing and the courage to resist. And one must never do this work alone, but always among like-minded scholars who can provide deep and abiding support.

Perhaps a discussion of Cone's legacy (alongside other stories of resistance) is the new conversation scholars and students of color must have in order to resist the desire to pass.

3

The Blessings and Burdens
of Black Theological Education

In 2009, I arrived at Brite Divinity School as a tenure-track professor—and the director of black church studies (BCS). As the only African American on faculty when I arrived, I took this directorship in part to ensure that I had some control over what the identity of this program would be—though my energies were so bound up with achieving tenure that in advance I had no idea what I was going to do with the program. I quickly realized I needed to figure it out if I was going to provide excellent theological formation for black students at Brite. I got to work.

That first week, a student I will call Joyce walked through my office door, sat down, and shared the anxieties she felt about the BCS program as a queer black woman. Joyce was all too aware of how many black churches and black seminaries interpret blackness in reductive ways that do not make room for a plurality of black identities. She shared with me her history of trauma, a trauma that she constantly encountered in black churches as a queer woman. Thinking academic spaces would be a safe haven to think through questions of sexual oppression, she had arrived at seminary, only to discover that her sexual identity often remained invisible and peripheral within the academic context, even among black faculty. To be part of the program, she needed to trust how I envisioned the purposes and aims of the program, specifically whether I planned to shape a black theological model that could address these urgent concerns. She was nervous yet hopeful.

As Joyce left my office, I had no inkling of the controversy that would erupt in the program I was leading. In this chapter, I share a story that reveals some of the paradoxes of black theological education. While the BCS program at Brite is quite different than that offered at a black seminary, I want to meditate on the ongoing tensions and contradictions of black theological education for native daughters and sons who are often rendered invisible (black women and black queer folks), even as I foreground the gifts black theological education brings for envisioning alternate futures for the theological academy. Native daughters and sons experience themselves as insiders and outsiders of black theological education as well.

* * *

My own racial formation as a black scholar is paradoxical and complex. Having attended a primarily white academy for most of my childhood, I arrived in 1998 at Tennessee State University (TSU) in Nashville, one of many excellent historically black colleges and universities (HBCUs). This is where I found my voice. Prior to TSU, I knew very little black history or what my contribution could be as a black woman in America. Reflections on racial identity were simply not on my radar. In fact, such discussions were discouraged or evaded altogether at my childhood school, whose white leaders felt their own clumsiness and confusion about how to approach the question of race. Instead, they gestured at their ideal of a postracial, color-blind society and assumed that Christian identity transcended racial identity. Although I had had experiences that reminded me of the trauma of racial aggression, even as a black girl in that context I understood race as a thing of the past, not something that shaped current social or religious identities in this country.

On arriving at the first-year women's dorm Wilson Hall, I was immediately captivated by the presence of so many young black women, full of excitement and vision for where their futures might take them. Although I had not yet been introduced to the term "womanist," this dorm experience initiated me into a community of young black women who practiced mutuality and deep care. Some of my newfound friends had a different view of the world than I did, and they opened my eyes to the multiple ways in which black women embody brilliance and resilience in the face of racism, patriarchy, and other forms of aggression. These women were my sisters, and we dreamed about our futures together. These women and TSU changed how I understood myself as a black woman navigating the world, and how I could use my gifts to pursue a vocation of justice to improve the lives of my own communities.

Wilson Hall was my beginning, but the theater program at TSU is where I was born again. That I had won a number of oratorical competitions in my hometown prepared me to experiment with live theater, where I found my muse: Lorraine Hansberry. Hansberry was more than simply a historical playwright to me; she was a poet, a critic, an American prophet. She challenged me to think more deeply about problems of racial, gender, and class injustice. Reading Hansberry was like holding sacred water—a refreshing and rejuvenating experience, but one that always eluded my grasp. The way her words, thoughts, and feelings moved through my soul reminded me of my own gloriously fragile life in this world. I wanted to speak the truth like Lorraine.

I remember receiving the role of a lifetime—the character Beneatha in Hansberry's play *A Raisin in the Sun*. Hansberry's letters and other political works make it clear that Beneatha reflected much of Lorraine Hansberry's own personality and commitments.[1] Beneatha was unapologetically opinionated as a young black woman; at nineteen, I was hesitant and always somewhat concerned about how my opinions were received by others. Beneatha was edgy and avant-garde; I was rather compliant and found solace in the traditions in which I grew up. Beneatha was a radical feminist, fully aware and self-possessed in her sexuality; I was scared of my own sexual awakening and felt shame for the free woman I *wanted* to become. But it was through playing Beneatha that I came into black feminist consciousness. The audience watches as Beneatha reclaims African culture through clothing and dance; as Beneatha speaks in other languages to combat the stereotype that black women lack intellect and brilliance; as Beneatha refuses to let the men in her life determine her own agency. It was through inhabiting the role of Beneatha that I slowly began walking away from the role of the dutiful daughter. Whereas before taking this role I hid who I truly was under the mask of who I thought people expected me to be, playing Beneatha enabled me finally to inhabit myself—a black woman who could speak truthfully about the world around me, a world characterized not only by racial and sexist animus and violence but also by black women's beautiful capacity to resist, to dream radical visions with their minds and hearts as well as build new worlds with their own hands. I was transformed.

I immersed myself in Lorraine's life and found her letters and writings in *To Be Young, Gifted and Black* amazing. I read it like scripture, reading line by line, pausing to meditate, to glean some new insight that I could apply to my life. Although we were on very different trajectories vocationally, I did feel this one resonance with her: the need to write to express my growing activist call. I began writing and performing short one-woman plays that reflected on major historical and social injustices from a feminist standpoint, such as the raping of black women during slavery, the experience of rape among Native American women during the trails of tears, and more. I felt a pull to write other women of color into existence who could tell their stories of oppression and resistance. It was glorious. And it initiated a process of formation for me that would shape me over and over again, from graduate work to my intellectual life as a professor in theological education.

These experiences awakened my sense of agency to claim my voice as a black woman in order to lead the communities I loved so much. I experienced this radical formation through the arts at an HBCU. Who I am is because of this context. These institutions have tremendous historical legacies. And I represent the best of the HBCU tradition.

Given the structural racism that black students endure in white theological spaces, why don't these students opt out of white contexts altogether? Why endure such racial assault and micro-aggressions? Why confront the exhausting threat of learning to pass when HBCU institutions remain available to attend? Why don't black students simply go to HBCU seminaries or divinity schools? Some of our best black theological voices were shaped by these institutions, among them Dr. Katie Geneva Cannon (Barber-Scotia College and Johnson C. Smith Seminary). Why is it assumed that Cannon's black and womanist sensibilities were primarily (or even solely) shaped at Union Theological Seminary? What about the fact that she received her BA and MDiv from black institutions? Does it matter that she discusses her deep theological shaping in blackness prior to arriving at Union? Certainly Union Seminary framed and fashioned her intellectual trajectory as a womanist foremother and scholar. But note how these black institutions that deeply formed her are rendered almost invisible in others' accounts of her religious and intellectual formation. Why is this? Black institutions remain invaluable for so many black scholars, helping us come into voice in order to engage the world.

* * *

Black institutions and even black educational spaces within predominantly white institutions (PWIs) are incredibly important for black faculty and students, but they are not without deep contradictions and flaws. I will never forget the controversy that ensued around me as the director of Brite's BCS program in relation to an annual symposium. I inherited an advisory board for this program when I arrived at Brite, some members of which were deeply supportive of my vision (such as Revs. Walter McDonald, Carol Gibson, Reuben Thompson, and Freddy Haynes) and others who were not. During my first three years, the BCS advisory board (made up of various black clergypersons from the Fort Worth area) and I put together an annual symposium on urgent issues facing black churches. This symposium was a community-wide event to encourage conversations between black academics and black practitioners on questions of justice and flourishing for black communities. I loved watching diverse lay leaders and clergy gather to learn more about the issues that directly affected the communities they served. One particular year, I wanted to foreground the problem of hetero-patriarchy and sexism in the black church.

The composition of the panel at the symposium was primarily women. A number of participants talked directly about the gross sexism black women have experienced in church contexts and how lingering patriarchal practices prevent truthful discussions about gender violence within these spaces. Some women panelists talked about broader issues such as human trafficking and domestic violence. One panelist directly critiqued the misogyny that undergirds the messages of well-known megachurch pastors in Dallas. Most provocatively, a couple of the women panelists urged black men to reexamine a number of historical male idols (e.g., Martin Luther King Jr.) who are often lauded without *any* discussion of the unhealthy biases and actions these leaders embodied that maintained entire systems of gender oppression within black communities. It was one of the best conversations I have facilitated between the black academy and broader black community. But not everyone thought it was a success.

Immediately after the symposium, a few of Brite's board members contacted me, perturbed about the symposium. I wasn't upset over the fact that we disagreed about the success of the symposium, for creative conflict should be a part of any well-functioning community. What bothered me was their primary claim about *why* the symposium was a problem. For some of the board members, the problem was uneven representation on the symposium panel. Some were angry because the panel was almost all women. I was stunned. How many times have events associated with the black church or black academy had panels or preacher rosters that were exclusively male? Shouldn't we *want* to hear from those who bear the burden and moral cost of sexism and patriarchy within black churches? I found particularly stunning that black male and female pastors on the board were part of the disgruntled chorus about the absence of black male representation on this panel.

Sometimes women themselves reinforce patriarchy.

As I reflected on the situation more calmly, I realized that the makeup of the panel was only the identified problem, not the real one. The real problem for a few of these board members was that panel members had challenged black patriarchy in black churches, even naming black pastors in the Dallas area, a move that a couple of the board members could not stomach. But to address hetero-patriarchy, you have to "undress" it, reveal how it reproduces an entire culture of silence and marginalization.

Then a board member resigned, and an advisory board meeting was called to reiterate to me the "problem." I realized that I did not share the same vision of black theological education and the future of the black church as some board members (not all of them—the majority were deeply supportive of my vision and, by extension, Brite's vision). I understand why some board members objected to what they perceived to be the radical character of the symposium. They felt this BCS program should stay focused on the quest for racial justice—gender and sexuality are too contested and not the main issues. Theirs is, after all, a familiar response.

Four decades ago, the task of black theological education was primarily about foregrounding racial justice as central to Christian witness and identity. Consider Miles Jones, who in 1972 penned an article for the *Christian Century* entitled "Why a Black Seminary?" He states that black seminaries provide a kind of theological formation that the "state cannot license."[2] This "state cannot license" claim must be read against the problem of institutional racism upheld by American political institutions. The American state (legal, juridical, social, and economic institutions) grounded the antiblack character of religious contexts such as US churches and seminaries. Most seminaries completely ignored or dismissed this racist reality. Consequently, black theological education is not merely challenging white ecclesial ideologies and practices but also challenging the state in which much of white religious practice gains its political sustenance and strength. For Jones, there will be a need for black theological schools as "long as there are black reality and white ignorance concerning that reality."[3]

The board members that were angry would resonate with this analysis. And I do as well. However, this discussion operates as blessing *and* burden, for it doesn't get at the *intersectional* realities that frame experiences of race in America and how folks such as black women and black same-gender-loving people navigate the injustices associated with the black church and broader society. It was clear that some of these board members did not want to wrestle with and be transparent about their own patriarchy and homophobia, as they resisted altogether the kinds of questions black hetero-patriarchy raised for them within their own ministerial contexts. Problems of racial injustice are not the only problems black women and black LGBTQ people face. And black theological education needs to reflect this complex reality.

That wasn't the last controversy in which I was embroiled. Another controversy centered around how to engage black LGBTQ students within the BCS program. Brite is an educational oasis in a southern region marked by deep Christian conservatism. Many seminaries in the Dallas area do not support the ordination or leadership of women in the church. They are also adamant in rejecting the inclusion of LGBTQ persons into ministry leadership. This traditional religious and cultural ethos in the Dallas area (and surrounding towns) makes it very difficult for women and queer students who are called into ministerial leadership. I remember a few black women students from Dallas Theological Seminary (DTS) contacting me about mentoring them while enrolled at DTS. It was hard to communicate to these women that mentorship from me would be somewhat challenging if they remained in a toxic educational context that did not support who they were as women called to religious leadership. Such conversations were often heartbreaking, as these students wrestled with whether and how they could stay loyal to their childhood traditions in the face of these traditions that dismissed their vocational identities. Brite was different. It categorically supported women and LGBTQ individuals in envisioning what it means to be the church and embody the gospel of radical love and inclusion while staying faithful to their own denominational contexts.

When I arrived at Brite, I assumed that anyone serving on the BCS advisory board would embrace these central and basic theological commitments. Yet when I planned another panel discussion about the state of the black church that would include the voices of black women and black LGBTQ persons, an advisory board member approached me and insisted that the gay students should establish an LGBTQ program to deal with "their issues" so that the BCS program could maintain its focus on black issues. I was taken aback. To *which* blacks does the BCS program belong? It was clear to me that this board member felt that black LGBTQ experiences are *not* part of the black experience and therefore have nothing to share about the black condition in the church or broader society. To this member, the BCS program essentially belonged to cis-gendered, heterosexual black men and their experiences of racism. As a black woman, this was a problem to me. After I disagreed with this suggestion, I was met with yet another resignation. I knew that there was a basic disagreement over theological values between me and some of the board members, a disagreement that centered around whose voice and experience counted within the black community, the black church, and by extension, black theological education.

Black male voices are often treated as if they are the representative voices on the meanings and ends of the black theological enterprise. Certainly they have something to contribute, but they are often treated as if they are the sole authority. This is what angered these black male board members so much: I would not submit to their idea of what needed to be privileged in training black students for ministry and broader work in society. Refusing to acquiesce in the face of these clergy leaders pushed me to reflect more deeply about the futures of black churches. So many black churches are unwilling to have transparent conversations about gender and sexual inclusion. In the church tradition of my childhood, they have refused to revisit a national discussion on women's ordination. This refusal has also led to a plethora of black women who grew up in COGIC pastoring in other denominations. Imagine the loss of wisdom and institutional insight COGIC has sustained because official leaders refuse to honor the calls and gifts of its own native daughters. That refusal is causing an entire generation to be suspicious of black churches and their theological conservatism because this conservatism causes trauma and exclusion.

The impact this kind of fighting had on my desire to engage the advisory board was unfortunate. For I could not meaningfully wrestle with this dynamic without putting my tenure in jeopardy. I needed energy and time to allocate to my writing, and for that I had to be psychologically healthy. I made a conscious choice to guard my energy. However, I recognize that this "guarding" of my energy did not always translate in life-giving ways to those on the board who truly supported me and the larger institution. These experiences caused me to doubt the usefulness of the board itself, creating distance between me and the entire board. Trauma within community affects us all in ways that exceed easy blame. My youthful energy and hope about what I could accomplish with an advisory board on arriving at Brite had bumped into reality. There is a cost to taking on old black church paradigms. And this cost marked me in ways that spawned both pride and sadness. That experience made me wonder how many black women or black same-gender-loving persons are depleted from trying to invite black clergypersons to wrestle with the marginalization of black women and black LGBTQ folks within black communities and black churches. How do we hold on to our integrity and joy as we work to build more just, loving worlds?

Black women scholars in theological education have been addressing this question for several decades. Womanist theologian Delores Williams published an essay in 1978 that identifies a gap, a structural problem located in both white and black seminaries. She reflects on the question of gender parity at a time when the battle lines were drawn on women's ordination. In reflecting on her experience at Union Theological Seminary as a professor, she imagines black women being treated as real subjects of theological education, as agents who can shape how a theological institution might understand its mission, aims, and end goals. What do black women need as students at Union? "We need role models. We need competent scholars who are black women. We need black women to provide input into the selection process. We need to select our own voices to represent us in those processes. . . . We need spiritual community and financial support to structure whatever it takes to make our academic experience here compatible with our vocational objectives and with our personal needs as students. We need the facilities to enter into those self-definition processes which help us understand more fully our ministry to the world."[4] Williams offered a prophetic critique of both white and black theological education.

Formation sits at the heart of the theological enterprise. But students cannot be formed and shaped if, from the start, the institutional orientation *disallows* self-definition to emerge. For Williams, taking seriously black women as subjects is about inclusion—but not *only* about inclusion. Taking seriously black women as subjects and agents reshapes the ways a diversity of students are invited into the "self-definition processes" of theological education in order to discern their own unique callings and tasks. This is what some of the BCS board members missed. One does not need to agree with the perspective or "lifestyle" of others to give them room to self-define who they will be and what life purpose they will embody. All seminarians, black students included, come from different walks of life and diverse Christian traditions. Being able to have authentic dialogue about these diverse pathways empowers students to choose who they will be. These few board members wanted to choose for these students, based on dogmatic, absolutist views about God and the world. This posture is violent and fails to treat people who are different from oneself as *definers* of their own vocational futures.

I was asking BCS board members at Brite to take seriously black women and black queer people as *subjects* who deserve to define their own vocational trajectories inside of black church studies programs. This kind of open invitation to the *free* formation of vocational identity enlarges and enriches the work of theological institutions and churches, which has ramifications for black women but more broadly for any marginalized group that experiences repression within theological education.

Black theological education expresses this central paradox: that although it has provided liberatory contexts for theological thought and praxis, it has simultaneously been a center of profound exclusion and violence. Some black women and queer folks experience themselves as insiders and outsiders within black theological education. Katie Cannon addresses this paradox and offers a way of thinking beyond these dangers of theological education within white and black institutions alike. In a superbly witty, insightful, and brilliant 1992 essay, she wrote about the value of womanist pedagogy for institutional change within theological education. The pedagogical metaphor she offers to challenge patriarchy in white and black seminaries intrigues me. She asserts that in order to crack open the patriarchal traditions that underlie theological institutions and Christian practices, black women scholars must "work with our sleeves rolled up, busily sharpening our oyster knives."[5] Oyster knives break open what desires to stay concealed and inaccessible. This is how intersectional oppressions such as racism and patriarchy often operate. Institutions do not want people to crack the code and expose the interior life of their structural pathologies. Because to break open patriarchal traditions is to map out how they might be resisted and dismantled, taking away their inevitability and even enchantment. I like to imagine that over many years Williams and Cannon were busy sharpening their oyster knives within the context of theological education and teaching others to do the same, asking how we might open up black theological education and the theological academy more broadly to different futures.

After encountering the controversies in the BCS program, I realized that many black clergypersons often freeze-frame particular experiences they hold as normative and standard. In the white theological context, the subject that tends to be centered is the white, cis-gendered, heterosexual man seeking ordination. In black theological education, it tends to be the black, cis-gendered, heterosexual man. These are the subjects that speak of the human experience (white men) or black experience (black men). This presents an epistemological problem: the knowledge production process itself is in the hands of men. We are unable to move forward and envision new futures in theological education because the categories that frame the meanings of the enterprise disallow new modes of being, knowing, and doing on which marginalized people (including women and queer folks) are already reflecting.

In "Metalogues and Dialogues: Teaching the Womanist Idea," Cannon insists that new educational futures are possible only when we move beyond the *content* of theological education to address the *form* and *structure* of theological education. For Cannon, black women scholars help reset how we think about the *epistemological* shape of theological education itself. Cannon insists that we must seek more than inclusion (the politics of social recognition) in relation to the content of theological education. We desperately need to arrive at new understandings of our doing, knowing, and being within our institutional context. In her words, it's not *just* thinking about "a territory to be covered" (much like some black male scholars assert in which the inclusion of black ideas or racial justice is the sole task);[6] more deeply, it's about discerning the kind of compass we need that can point us in ever-expanding directions in relation to knowledges and practices within diverse communities.[7] For this task, the journey is as important as the destination, as one learns so much about the landscape en route to where one is going. This also opens up possibilities of taking many different routes, of exploring new territories and different terrains that one did not even know existed. And the expansion of knowledge about new territories opens up the possibility for new journeys. In other words, new journeys alter the form of knowledge itself—and yield surprising discoveries and possibilities that we may not have anticipated.

This is what Cannon refers to as metalogues, a dialogical paradigm of where theological education needs to go among white and black seminaries. A metalogue reflects on how we do dialogue from a "meta-level." It asks how openness to diverse perspectives through dialogue reshapes the form and structure of knowledge itself. Metalogues focus on how we attune ourselves to the gaps, silences, and blind spots. Yet this attunement only comes within the matrix of interaction with others. For Cannon, a metalogic direction for theological education compels us to ask how even our most radical pedagogies might be missing something and how the search for that something, in each new iteration, reshapes content and structure of theological education itself. So *we just can't work back from the telos*, because the telos might be taking new shapes and forms depending on new knowledges and practices that are constantly emerging in a rapidly shifting world. *This* is what black theological education has often missed because it mimics the hetero-patriarchal hierarchy of white theological education: that something might be missing from our theological education because diverse experiences are locked out and unable to dislodge the epistemological and ethical center.

We can see that this metalogic orientation encourages us to explore the relationship between knowledges and ecology—how the ecological environments we foster (the kind of habits and virtues of mind and behavior) shape the form of the knowledges we hold dear. When our ecologies are marked by racial and gender distortions, our knowledges bear this rigidity and are unable to open out into the diversity of experiences that mark God's expansive creation. When our ecologies are marked by openness, new knowledges and practices can emerge. This is what is at stake not just for white seminaries but for black seminaries, for black theological education. Cannon gives us a gift in this essay—a way to think about the future of theological education by turning to the importance of institutional ecology in rethinking new forms of knowledge and practice. We do well to heed her prophetic call to action.

As native daughter, I recognize that black theological education is not necessarily *the* final answer to the structural racism of white theological spaces. Some black scholars may feel this way, but I do not. I testify about my experiences at Brite to highlight the contradictions and complexities of black theological programs. As a black woman, I battled inside of these black spaces, refusing the hetero-patriarchal practices of black churches. I also have seen how black queer people are treated in black educational spaces, even as these spaces prove to be resourceful for their theological journey. Black theological education possesses a paradox, as it is both liberating and repressive, emancipatory and limiting. I live in this tension as a native daughter who believes in the power of black theological education yet acknowledges its faults and frailties.

* * *

This question of representative voices in black theological education is crucial to hearing native daughters and sons. While leading the BCS program, I largely wanted to create educational options *for black students who were being missed by white and black theological spaces*. Particularly, black LGBTQ individuals are often met with a paucity of educational options within white and black seminary contexts alike, locked out of many church structures (which can also mean funding for attending seminary) and often experiencing cycles of financial and social deprivation because of their sexual identity.

I focused my administrative energy on the ongoing *question of access among black students, especially black women and black queer folks.* The question of access should shape pedagogical commitments within institutions. Yet this matter of access is contested terrain. I saw this play out while I was a professor at Brite. Before I arrived, Brite initiated evening courses as a way to encourage more bivocational students to enroll, particularly working-class students. Eventually, this evening-course structure was applied across all course requirements, which meant that each professor was required to teach an evening course at least every two years. The hope was to attract more students to Brite who traditionally would be unable to enroll. This change certainly met with resistance.

Some professors were irritated by or outright opposed to teaching evening courses. I was one of these professors! Some faculty members argued that they rarely got the best work from students at night. Students often came to class tired after working a full-time job during the day. These evening students often showed signs of exhaustion and at times were unable to keep up with the requirements of the course itself (such as readings or assigned projects). I certainly remember students struggling as they navigated daytime jobs and academic obligations. Moreover, some professors simply disliked evening courses because they themselves were not at their most intellectually alert then. Certainly that is how I felt at first. I was not convinced about the virtues of offering evening courses.

That changed when I met a student I will call Chris. He could not be a traditional full-time student during the day due to his job. Chris was a clergyperson and activist within the LGBTQ community. As he progressed through the class, I became more aware of his many commitments. Chris had a deep desire to embark on the journey of theological education, especially as a black same-gender-loving man. I was clear that theological education was critically important to him and his growing sense of vocational identity. In addition to being a pastor and activist in the local Dallas area, he was also a regional bishop associated with a larger network of churches, the Fellowship of Affirming Ministries (TFAM). Founded and led by Bishop Yvette Flunder, TFAM has been at the forefront of ministerial advocacy not only for LGBTQ affirmation and inclusion but also for other marginalized groups who are excluded within society, such as poor people and immigrants. Through TFAM, Chris's ministerial work was at a regional and national level. I was intrigued by the work he was doing, both in itself and because it reflected the growing edges of my own work and the broader academy's mission. There was something *Chris could teach me* about theological education.

Chris changed me. Listening to him talk about his unique challenges shed light on why it was so important for the seminary to have evening courses as well as why theological education needs to undergo massive reconstruction. I watched as Chris balanced his academic assignments with his leadership within the LGBTQ community, work in which he endured daily assaults. It wasn't so much that Chris talked about his struggles of ministry and academic life; I saw the struggle through his body language when he entered the classroom after a hard, stressful week. I saw the struggle in how he grasped for time to grow intellectually in the midst of the people he served, who often faced severe life-and-death issues. I remember asking myself what theological education could offer him.

Professors often talk about ideal students as the ones who meet every deadline, write stellar academic papers (normally theoretically and philosophically cogent), and know how to participate in class discussions. Yet, this is the imaginary student based on the traditional model of theological education—young, unmarried, with no children, and able to devote himself or herself full time and singularly to study. This was not Chris's profile. In foregrounding the needs of nontraditional students, I am not asserting that institutions should lower their standards or allow mediocre work. Instead, I am inviting institutions to think about what we hold as valuable to vocational formation and growth and to think about the diverse kinds of academic work that empower students to cultivate their own forms of leadership. Outstanding paper writing is valuable but cannot measure or show how successful students will be as leaders in nonprofit, pastoral, or even activist work.

Chris made far more of an impact on me than any other student I have taught. This is the dilemma that Chris raises for theological education: Will theological models acknowledge that Chris is the student of the present and future? Can we rethink our assumptions about who is enrolling in our theological institutions? A number of students nowadays cannot attend school full time (or are bivocational), which means that we professors must expand our understanding of why we teach and embrace different ways of teaching and learning. Access is key so that diverse voices can flourish. We need theological and institutional creativity in rethinking our models, but this means our traditional notions of the ideal student must die.

* * *

While the director of the BCS program at Brite, I wanted to address the question of formation. Many black students come to get more than information: they come to be formed theologically and spiritually. Becoming a confessionally oriented theological leader is the goal of many black seminarians and divinity students. They want to testify about their own experiences of God and put those experiences in conversation with theological discourses in order to be shaped and formed as a more faithful Christian leader. In the black church, formation has long been central. But whereas in the past we could count on the black church to instill in people values such as communal solidarity and responsibility along with accountability to poorer black communities, now some black churches embrace a more capitalist, individualistic mind-set and practice. I talk about this in my book *Unfinished Business*. In the middle of the twentieth century, with greater economic mobility among more black people, such communities wanted to legitimate their growing economic attainment. They did this through religious ideology. Their social and economic achievements, they said, were the result of God's favor. There is a long history in this country of ascribing wealth and social status to divine favor. African Americans began embracing this Puritan idea, which had implications for black churches. One of the negative implications was that black Christians stopped believing they had a duty toward those who were economically disadvantaged in their communities. Black church members also often default to intensely personal accounts of salvation, without exploring the broader social character of their Christian witness. This has led to malformation in some black churches, which compels a number of black students to seek out seminary contexts. They want to enlarge what it means to be Christian.

The power of black theological institutions is that students can bring their confessional selves to theological study without fear or hesitancy. In many mainstream white liberal theological spaces (especially those associated with universities), senior scholars are suspicious of confessional dispositions. However, a number of students show up at seminary or divinity school wanting to explore how their various confessional stances can be critiqued and refined through theological scholarship. They do not desire to compartmentalize themselves, separating their confessional lives from their intellectual lives. Many students in the academy see themselves as scholar-preachers or scholar-pastors who are committed to seeing faith and intellect as complementary rather than oppositional, or at least frictional but never antagonistic.

Within black theological education, this ability to claim and pursue confessional praxis has been its strength. Indeed, HBCU divinity schools and seminaries (as well as black church studies programs in predominantly white institutions) pride themselves on intentionally shaping students of faith, students who wrestle with theological questions within the context of their own Christian communities, whether Baptist, Methodist, or Pentecostal. As dean of the 2017 Samuel Dewitt Proctor Conference seminary gathering, I remember engaging students from both Howard Divinity School and Virginia Union. Their comfort with bringing their full confessional selves to theological education was palpable. On the other hand, having taught in two predominantly white seminaries/divinity schools, I know firsthand the ways black students struggle with formation because they feel they are unable to be both confessional and critical thinkers within these theological contexts.

All HBCU seminaries/divinity schools and black church studies programs (in white theological institutions) are unapologetically linked to black churches. For some people, that may be a problem. At times, black churches are slower to embrace, and may even create obstacles to, diverse black freedom struggles such as gender equality for black women or sexual inclusion among black LGBTQI persons. Some academic leaders feel these institutions impede rather than sponsor black thriving across multiple black Americas. As stated earlier, my childhood church tradition, the largest black denomination in the country, still refuses to ordain women. How can black churches talk about gender parity for black women in our country when they deny black women an opportunity to lead beside men within their own ecclesial contexts? The outright hypocrisy of black churches makes it hard for some scholars to support seminaries or divinity schools that are beholden to these institutions.

But I want to make a case that black churches have something to *offer* theological education. Black churches still exert tremendous influence within black communities and within black popular culture, which means that black churches should be engaged rather than avoided. Consider the large black following (both in and outside the black church) that Tyler Perry movies have. His movies, featuring the sarcastic, older, tell-it-like-it-is Mabel "Madea" Williams, draw millions of black viewers, many of whom are in the black church world. One might say that Perry preaches from his own media pulpit and allows people to go to church right in their living rooms, even though his work often reinforces a highly sexist institutional gaze. One might disagree with how, for example, Perry depicts black women in his movies, but his impact on the black cultural imagination cannot be denied. This is what HBCU divinity schools and seminaries understand about black churches: that black students come through the seminary doors shaped by their respective church contexts and therefore must be engaged from *within* those very contexts, not from outside of them. Moreover, a number of black churches are in the vanguard for economic, racial, gender, and sexual justice. I strongly dislike people making statements about *the* black church, as if it were a monolithic institution. There is a diversity of black churches, and some are leading the way in envisioning truly inclusive futures for black communities and broader society.

* * *

Although I have now moved on to Princeton as a professor, had I remained at Brite as the director of the BCS program, I would have wanted to foreground new centers of black theological formation that can be more welcoming to native daughters and sons. One example of such formation can be seen in the emergence of radical black Pentecostalism(s). The historical emergence and contemporary reconfiguration of Pentecostalism in the United States and around the world are something that the theological academy must take seriously and engage for two reasons: first, because there is a sharp increase in students of Pentecostal or charismatic backgrounds attending seminaries and divinity schools, and second, because Pentecostalism is reshaping Christian faith in the United States and around the world, and this should compel us to think about what this means for Christian practice and theological education. In addition, new black Pentecostalism(s) are emerging in the United States, forms of Pentecostal faith that are profoundly subversive and countercultural. I am interested in how these new black Pentecostalism(s) can be gifts to imagining otherwise futures in theological education.

In 2018, the Samuel Dewitt Proctor School of Theology at Virginia Union University established a Center for Afro-Pentecostalism to respond to the growing number of Pentecostal and neo-Pentecostal students enrolling in their theological institution. This center was established to celebrate, explore, and communicate the African American Pentecostal heritage and its theological traditions. This statement challenges merely using Pentecostal students as tokens of religious or Christian diversity. Whenever administrators and senior faculty members have conversations about student diversity, they rarely move beyond how such diversity improves the optics of the institution. I have watched as theological schools that have only five or ten black students saturate their institutional advertisement with black and brown faces, as if this image were a true representation of the school's demographic makeup. Many students who arrive at the school are shocked and disappointed at the lack of diversity in student and faculty population. They feel the institution has lied. (And it has.)

Another form of tokenism is when an impressive black student is asked to participate in every event and be on every public panel. The student must be able to "pass" intellectually, that is, be someone white administrators and faculty feel comfortable engaging. Black faculty encounter this same problem. The tenured or pretenure black faculty member is asked to sit on multiple governance committees, search committees, and task forces that may address diversity in some way. Some black faculty are even expected to be "team players" and direct school programs that focus on the needs of black students or students of color. This leads to exhaustion and burnout. Such overwhelming expectations cripple whatever creativity of teaching and writing scholars of color may bring with them to their institutional context. Students and scholars of color who represent a racial or religious diversity should not be engaged for the sake of mere utility. Their presence is not simply to serve the interests of institution building and media optics. And likewise, students with Pentecostal backgrounds do not come to seminary to be treated as tokens by institutions who desire to be seen as inclusive and diverse.

Instead, celebrating black Pentecostal heritage means making a bold claim: to be Christian *is* to be Pentecostal. Black Pentecostalism has something to teach the white and black theological academy, although it is often treated as a fringe or insignificant movement outside of broader Christian faith. However, this is far from the truth. While Pentecostalism has multiple origins around the world, I am compelled by the religious life of the Azusa Street Revival of 1906. Begun in Los Angeles by an African American itinerant preacher, William Seymour, and a group of black washerwomen and domestics, the Azusa Street Revival certainly included *glossolalia* (speaking in tongues) and mystical acts such as healing. But this movement also understood Christian faith to be enacted and lived out in community through transgressing and subverting the racist, sexist, and classist *habitus* of American culture and economy at the dawn of the twentieth century. Various biographers and testimonial narratives speak about Azusa "washing away the color line" in the "blood of the Lamb" through black, white, Latinx, Irish, Italian, Armenian, and other people worshiping and living together in radical community. Now, for certain, the statement that "Azusa washed the color line away in the blood of the Lamb" is highly contestable even among those writing about the meanings of Azusa in 1906. However, the archives associated with the Azusa revival interpret this ongoing community as deeply engaged in a form of political agency that is actualized in and through their religious life, a religious life that rejected the false promise of modern American institutions that failed to provide democracy, equal citizenship, and equity.

Although Azusa members did not appeal to the state apparatus to overturn formal US racist laws and patriarchal codes, those associated with the Azusa revival did embody a political agency that defied the current social and cultural order through individuals of different races and ethnicities worshiping and eating together as well as through gender parity in church leadership. However, some scholars describe Azusa's religious life as primarily oriented toward otherworldly (apocalyptic) dimensions. They choose to focus primarily on its practices of speaking in tongues or healing to the exclusion of its embodiment of a subversive community that stands as an affront to the segregationist order of that era. For them, Azusa is simply *apolitical*. But these critics are wrong. They miss the political significance of Azusa because they miss the ways Azusa redefined what counts as political.

Early Pentecostalism at Azusa is perhaps the most poignant example of prophetic Christianity at the dawn of the twentieth century. Azusa embodied countercultural practices in relation to America's racial, ethnic, patriarchal, and class hegemony. For instance, Azusa was subversive to the dominant racial reasoning of the day as seen through a 1906 political cartoon that depicts white women in the arms of salivating black men at the altar, with the headline, "Crazed White Girls in the Arms of Buck Black Men."[8] This was a dangerous headline. Black men could be lynched for even looking at a white woman—but Azusa was a context in which black men laid hands on (physically touching the heads of people while praying for them) white women, which was a scandalous practice for this era. Azusa reflected an interracial community, as a black clergyman, Seymour, alongside black washerwomen, led and pastored thousands of white Christians at Azusa. In terms of emancipatory gender norms, when the congregation organized itself, the twelve elders comprised five men and seven women.[9] The barriers of gender were very briefly overcome at Azusa, which contrasted with many of the Baptist and Methodist traditions at that time. Azusa was also a unique moment in the American religious landscape in terms of class, as most major religious movements (such as the Great Awakenings) in America certainly included black people but *were not started and led by poor black people, as Azusa was.* In its first three years, this revival's embodiment of communion, longing, and belonging across racial, gender, and class categories can be contrasted to the dominant ecclesial and juridical institutions of the day that stridently upheld racial apartheid and white superiority.

The legacy of Azusa is simply unknown by the majority of Christian denominations. Current Pentecostals often don't know their own history. I myself didn't learn this history until I was a seminary student in my early twenties. Pentecostalism is consequently often regarded as premodern, backward, primitive, overly emotional, and nonrational. This view dismisses or ignores the potential contribution of early Pentecostalism and contemporary progressive Pentecostalisms to the larger theological conversation. Some scholars have written that the most important contribution of early Pentecostalism has been the "revalorization of the charismata" rather than theological analysis. I think this is misguided. As seen at Azusa, Pentecostal spirituality and practice offer profound theological analysis. For in Pentecostal practice, it is only through the joining together of bodies in desiring, living with, and loving each other that Christian community is possible. Early Pentecostalism invites us to ask: How does Pentecostal religious experience revolutionize how we think about Christian identity and witness?

At Azusa Street, Christian identity was not based simply on *doctrinal agreement* but on *shared experiences* of the Spirit that were oriented toward intimate, loving, and just relations. To say that the Azusa revival had a low view of doctrine would be intellectually dishonest. But doctrine functioned more like theatrical instructions for a group of actors, and instructions can drastically change depending on the context and new dynamics that emerge among actors. This revival was highly experimental with forms of worship and spirituality, as well as flexible with people's basic core creeds. In fact, Seymour and other leaders were deeply suspicious of creeds associated with white churches, as they knew that creeds allowed white Christians to profess the tenets of Christianity while having racial hatred in their hearts (which inevitably fueled racist institutions). New religious experiences reshaped what they understood to be God's will and words to their community and broader world. Creedal commitments were constantly being revised at this revival. So while doctrine did shape Azusa's religious self-understanding, it was only *one* tool of discernment, not *the* tool of Christian identity and discernment. The main question was how God's Spirit was creating something new and previously impossible between people that had previously been at odds with each other. Azusa Street was not perfect (this community was plagued with many internal contradictions). But it did attempt to imagine and live into transgressive communities in response to the racist, hetero-patriarchal, and classist status quo.

The Spirit couldn't move abstractly. God's Spirit only moved in and through a community of bodies. The Spirit was felt among the Azusa congregants through touching, hearing, speaking, listening, eating, and embracing each other. The risk of the Azusa revival was the risk of touching and holding bodies that were taught to hate and fear each other: the white body repulsed by the black body; the white body held as suspicious by the immigrant body because of white xenophobia; the black body fearing the white body because of the violence and racial vitriol perpetrated against blacks. To announce oneself as Christian was to bring one's entire self, especially the body, near those who generated anxiety in oneself. To be Christian was not a statement but a performance with the body—touching, feeling, hugging, crying together at the altar or another part of the sanctuary or at someone's home as one encountered the Spirit. The Pentecostal encounter was a revolution of the intimate within the racial, gender, and class matrices of the United States. Azusa announced a different practice of the intimate.

Early Pentecostalism (as seen at Azusa) then compels us to ask how God's Spirit is manifested and revealed in and through the corporeal materiality of our lives as we move within our communities and institutional theological contexts. How does God's Spirit move in and through bodies of all races, ethnicities, nationalities, genders, and so forth in ways that anticipate the coming kin-dom? Reclaiming this less well-known history of early Pentecostalism is critically important for theological education. And part of that history is that African American leaders were at the heart of this revival and that a different way of relating, outside of the cycles of violence and trauma, was possible.

To connect the subversive character of early Pentecostalism with new, emerging forms of black Pentecostalism that are critiquing the status quo within churches and society today is likewise critically important. The Fellowship for Affirming Ministries (TFAM) is a multidenominational fellowship of primarily black churches that interpret the gospel as a theology and practice of radical inclusion and belonging similar to how the Azusa Street Mission did. For TFAM, radical inclusion is first an epistemological revolution in our own theologies. This in itself is ecclesially countercultural. Some Christian denominations operate with a logic of "insider/outsider" or "us versus them." The story goes something like this: to be a Christian means that other religious traditions are simply outside of God's will and redemptive plan. Or, to be gay means one has situated oneself as an enemy of the gospel, a heretic. This insider/outsider mentality is at the level of thought and feeling: our very ideas about what the gospel or Christian message *is* prevent us from thinking in more expansive, loving, and inclusive ways about who the church really is. Part of what TFAM seeks to do is rethink the true meanings of the gospel away from dogmatic interpretations of Christian life. While imperfectly striving to embody inclusive community, TFAM allows us to ask how we might cultivate radically welcoming communities, where people who have been previously ostracized and demonized are gathered together into the community of God.

What is interesting about TFAM is that it has a distinctively Pentecostal style of worship. The founder and presiding bishop, Yvette Flunder, comes out of COGIC and has deep intergenerational Pentecostal roots. In 2009, I experienced Flunder as the incarnation of an ideal I once thought impossible. I remember the scene like it happened yesterday. I was a new professor at Brite Divinity School. She was invited to preach at our weekly chapel service and engage our students around faith and sexuality. When she walked into the room, it felt like everything in the space was pulled to her very being. I could tell she was a seeker of truth, a Deborah who was clear about her spiritual leadership for this generation. As I sat there in chapel, molecules of joy, comfort, and power gathered around me. To see a black woman with deep roots in COGIC establishing an ecclesial movement dedicated to merging Pentecostal worship with critical, creative theology for marginalized people was shocking for me. I could feel her unapologetic witness from the time she sang to when she preached that morning—I was moved to tears. I wanted to know more about her, as I saw my own vocational identity deeply bound up with all that she was, and all that I wanted to be.

My pull toward her was not simply because of her undeniable, captivating presence. What compelled me was that her theological and vocational identity was not a mere echo of theological options already given for blacks in the academy, whether black Baptist or black Methodist. It wasn't Cone or Williams exactly. Not simply Martin or Rosa, nor Malcolm nor Angela. She was something different. She was a theological Shirley Caeser or Walter Hawkins. A James Cleveland or Lady Tramaine with a liberationist twist. The liturgical power of a Rance Allen but with a cutting-edge theology that sought to liberate the mind, body, and soul. Flunder embodied the full critique of her inherited Pentecostal tradition yet preserved and honored the "shout," the deep indigenous practices of Pentecostal worship that mediate the presence of God through the body, the joints, the wild dancing, the screams of deliverance, the cries of collective joy, and the testimonies that can only be heard through describing yourself as a witness to God's power. Her life testified and began fostering in me a new kind of theological space. She was a new moment for me and, I believe, an ongoing, emerging moment in the growing movement among progressive Pentecostals.

Her entire life affirms that to be Christian is to be Pentecostal. Her interpretation of Pentecost, which shapes her own movement (TFAM), points to her "village table" theology in which we should not merely acknowledge those on the edges of society but *gather* them in. In her book *Where the Edge Gathers: Building a Community of Radical Inclusion*, she offers theological and pastoral reflections on how religious leaders can create and cultivate practices of gathering. Using sermons and brief essays, she appeals to the ways in which Jesus was constantly gathering unlikely people and redefining what was possible for human community. In order to gather, we first have to be honest about the boundaries we must heed when we expose injustices, exploitation, and exclusion. All theological claims and practices are *not* equal—some are violently exclusive and must be resisted. In other words, lines of justice and care must be drawn when we are serious about truly acknowledging and loving the humanity of those who are marginalized and on the edges of society. I am aware that some institutions feel they can simply invite a diversity of perspectives on issues related to race, gender, and sexuality without being clear about their own institutional stance and gospel commitment on these matters. Part of gathering in people to create different, more liberating forms of intimacy and belonging means leaders must be clear about these boundaries— that leaders must be courageous in taking a stand with and for those who experience the weight of harm and trauma.

Yet I am also drawn to Flunder's insistence that hope does exist for radical belonging and embrace. For her, this is the heart of Pentecost. She is clear that practices of gathering are not just about acknowledging the excluded or ignored but are also about giving *everyone* a seat at the central meeting place or welcome table.[10] When I read this claim years ago, this was difficult for me to process and even accept. Does she mean everyone has a seat, including unrepentant racists or misogynists who see their exclusive theological perspectives as the will of God? No. After all, she is clear that Christian leaders must draw categorical lines on where they stand on issues of justice and belonging. When she speaks of "giving everyone a seat," she is envisioning a world where a new humanity is possible, where people can gather who once had no desire for each other, where people are not driven by the fear of the other but by their longing to experience belonging through the other, where oppressors can see the folly and harm caused by their sole commitment to abstract truths without assessing the contradictions those "truths" engender for those living inside of them, where those who are marginalized can live into a moment wherein conversion is possible for those who have harmed them, where this community of healing and belonging is the end of liberation rather than liberation being for its own sake. Flunder is dreaming into the eschatological promise of a new creation. This dreaming is not a naïve fantasy but a hopeful promise of community rooted in the life of the Spirit.

Flunder invites one to see healing, intimacy, belonging as something possible between previous oppressors and marginalized people. And she wants to make a bold proclamation: this is the Pentecost we must live into in this moment. She says this for a couple of reasons. First, we often draw easy distinctions between oppressor and oppressed, opting to ignore the complexities and ambiguities of identities—the ways in which someone can be oppressor and oppressed simultaneously. Hope for the conversion of someone else is also about hope in our own conversion—we who have been harmed and often produce harm. Second, Jesus's proclamation of the "good news" was not just about advocating justice for those who were silenced but the possibility of radical embrace among warring groups. We have a hard time gathering and creating more just and compassionate communities because we don't truly believe that another way of relating, of experiencing intimacy and belonging with each other across pain and trauma, exists.

This belief in another way of being is the heart of Pentecost, and theological educators, clergy, religious leaders, and Christians more generally must "see" this. Healing is possible, no matter how small the scale. Consider Flunder's sermon "The Conversion of a Pharisee." This sermon discusses the familiar conversion experience of Saul, a member of the religious elite who persecuted early Christians in order to preserve tradition and the status quo. I am drawn to what this sermon asks of us: Do we truly believe that conversion is possible of one who has done gross harm, and that those who have been traumatized can open their hearts to such a person in forming new relationships? This is a difficult question to ask because it seems to put the burden on the marginalized to make this community possible. This is fair. For example, I can see why some of the disciples such as Peter were deeply suspicious of Saul-turned-Paul, as he had been a holy crusader, killing Christians in the name of God. Why would they be motivated to embrace Paul within their burgeoning community? Their fear was justified. Or similar to Paul, recall the conversion of Cornelius, a Roman officer (who secures the Roman state) who seeks out Peter and stands before him as a potential new acolyte. This scene is both disturbing and deeply complex, as Cornelius was one soldier who made possible the occupation of the Jews. It says Cornelius was generally seen as a good man, yet he was still an outsider and a supporter of empire. Even so, he stood there with a desire for conversion. For certain, Acts 10 lets us know that Cornelius's conversion required something of him: turning away from the imperial project of Rome to be with and for this new community. It cost Cornelius *everything*—he could not continue to support the sinful structures of Rome if he desired to become part of this persecuted community. However, it is also clear that the Spirit takes Peter through a spiritual process in order to open up his heart to the possibility of a new kind of community with someone like Cornelius. This entire scene captures what it means to gather in unlikely persons. This is a radical and risky act. And it is deeply Pentecostal. This is the impossible possibility of the gospel.

As Jesus gathered and widened the community of faith, so too are we called to widen our understandings and practices of community. But this involves rethinking fixed tribal theologies. Instead, we need theologies that gather the edges of society, that center the marginalized and suffering in Christian faith and identity and make room for those who have harmed but experience true conversion. I want the theological academy to take note of black progressive Pentecostal leaders like Flunder who are doing the work of gathering and can teach us about our call to cultivate practices of gathering within contexts of theological education.

I am convinced that the futures of black theological education and indeed theological education as a whole can learn from what

Flunder and TFAM are doing. Yet TFAM is just one example of the kind of theological formation we need within white and black theological institutions and spaces. We need practices of gathering. We must gather native daughters and sons, allowing moments of conversion and embrace among unlikely people. I think radical Pentecostalisms have something to offer, although these Pentecostalisms are often overlooked within theological institutions. What would it mean to gather in ways that allow us truly to hear, see, and be with and for each other, which means sitting inside of the tension, conflict, anger, contradictions, and complexities of communal life itself? This would mean that native daughters would need room to testify to ongoing intersectional realities of oppression and trauma in order to make possible the cultivation of truly authentic spaces of healing and justice. White and black theological institutions must provide these spaces for native daughters to bear witness to these realities. We need to widen our practices of community so that we might be witnesses to a new otherwise way of being and living.

4

Becoming Undone

How might we think about deep renovations in theological education at the level of desire? Certainly scholars desire tenure and greater visibility in the theological academy. Administrators desire to balance the books and perpetuate institutional legacies or pedigrees. And students desire to leverage their degree to help them achieve certain ambitions. Yet amid all such desire we have learned neither to desire one another nor how to yearn for compassionate and just relations within our broken community. We often desire replicas of ourselves rather than others with whom we find ourselves in community. We have been blind to the fact that, at heart, the gospel is about the joining together of lives, of bodies, of desires to live and love and be transformed in and through each other. *We do not desire each other.*

How might we be witnesses to new forms of desire and togetherness marked by caring and just relations? In this concluding chapter, I offer words about the power of unlikely people being drawn together by deep yearnings to experience radical moments of intimacy and belonging. I recognize that talk about "desire" can easily slip into unhelpful didactic postures—me telling readers what they need to do in terms of their desires. My words do not seek to moralize in this way. I am not invested at all in offering neat and sanitized notions of desire, as if right desire were produced of one's own volition through simply better educating or disciplining one about others.

Instead, I offer my words as a lamentation and prayer. When I hear students and faculty of color in theological institutions remark that they do not trust white folks at all because of the structural trauma they have experienced, I lament. I do not lament because I think they are villainous for feeling this way. Racial pain produces suspicion and distrust. Rather, I lament because the racial violence that produces racial distrust doesn't make possible the joining together of lives that the gospel envisions. Likewise, when I see white students and faculty develop indifferent or antagonistic behavior toward stories of racial pain because they fear the guilt and responsibility associated with acknowledging racism and their own privilege, I lament. This entire scene produces an emotional economy of fear. New moments of radical intimacy and belonging are impossible.

And still I hope. I believe things can be different. I want to be a witness to this impossible possibility. But my hope is less in the form of liberal optimism and more in the form of a continued prayer. When I speak about the importance of unlikely people truly desiring each other and being drawn into radical community, I imagine my words meeting the reader as prayer rather than demand, as a meditation on "hoping against hope" rather than the expected nod toward liberal multiculturalism.

I don't have any final answers to the problems of theological education. But I am a witness. I am a witness to the power of radical intimacy and belonging among unlikely people, which can reshape the relational ecology of theological education. We need to experience the transformation of our desires to be with and for others. Without this desire, this yearning, and longing for something different than what we have, we are lost.

* * *

I have been part of a historical slavery audit at Princeton Theological Seminary. The audit offers a report on the seminary's complicity and benefit from the slave economy. It also involves recommending to the seminary's board of trustees an agenda of reparations for implementation. A large part of this process has been the multiple conversations we have had with students and alumni over this past year. The goal of the task force has been to empower the community to shape what repair or reparations should look like, particularly by listening to the voices of people of the African diaspora. I have been struck by how this audit created spaces at our school where black students and other students from nonwhite ethnic backgrounds could witness. A number of black students are naming what it feels like to read the report on Princeton's complicity during slavery and how these racist logics and practices continue to shape their experiences at our institution. They narrated many stories of racial trauma and pain that complicated their theological journeys at this place, in this community.

I do understand why some people might interpret this reparations agenda in pessimistic terms. White institutions have instrumentalized these kinds of agendas in order to be politically calculating in improving their reputations over racial issues. One might say that this kind of work is altruistic for all the wrong reasons. Because that's the easy route, I want to suspend this assumption when talking about the audit at Princeton. I think it's much more difficult to linger and meditate on the small but significant spaces for witnessing and vulnerability that students have experienced during this audit. These students did not describe the audit as perfect or even revolutionary, but they did speak about the significance of a series of small opportunities to form unlikely relationships and be witnesses about the racial tragedies they endure in church and society.

These audit conversations created surprising moments of intimacy among unlikely students. It was powerful to hear students (and even a couple of faculty members) talk about being vulnerable to each other. It was moving to hear black students speak at length about how they felt when hearing their white student colleagues confess and engage their complicity in conversations about ongoing structural racism. I was personally moved when students called a seven-day public prayer on the steps of the administration building in order to feel the power of community. I watched as this prayer group grew from under ten persons to well over thirty people on some days. More and more, I saw white students gather with the black seminarians to pray and talk about the importance of reparations as a Christian act of worship. One white student remarked to me that he was unsure about this call to reparations but was able to confess his own racial biases and white privilege as he witnessed the commitment to prayer that the black seminarians facilitated.

What arrested my attention was how students made room for small moments in which they could be undone by each other through practices of witnessing. At a town hall meeting, students had an opportunity to address the task force and trustees about the slavery audit report and the demand for reparations. The tension in the room was palpable. You could feel the sense of distrust that many students possessed in relation to the board and broader administration. As a task force member, I could sense the anger and frustration of black students, who were unsure whether the institutional agenda for reparations was merely a form of political expediency. There was a calm hum in the room when the meeting started, but this hum was laced with anticipated outcries.

I will never forget what I witnessed. Some trustees attended this meeting as an act of good faith. They wanted to assure the students that they were being as transparent and accountable as possible. Some students and faculty believed that this meeting was nothing more than managing growing concerns over the "next steps" of this audit. As soon as the meeting opened up, multiple students pressed the administration and board members on what institutional actions would be taken in light of Princeton's history of slavery. It was awkward at first. Students were demanding immediate concrete actions—a comprehensive agenda that the board could talk about right then to assuage the students' concerns. The conversation that ensued was expected, as board members were careful and measured about what they could say in light of any legal implications resulting from the institutional decisions they would make. The responses of some board members were slow, meticulous, and controlled. Students interpreted this as insincere.

Then one board member stood up and cleared the air. She named the elephant in the room. She conceded that the board members' responsibility is often the well-being and maintenance of the institution. Sometimes, certain institutional responsibilities and realities conflict with goals of justice and equity. Because board members must be vigilant concerning the legal ramifications of any institutional decision that is made, it makes transparency and vulnerability hard. She stood up and named this. To me, her action was risky, being vocally honest about this reality that often causes unending suspicion between administrations (often mostly white) and students of color.

But something else was at stake in her action. I could tell that her desire to respond to student cries for transparency arrested her at a deep emotional level. You could see it in her face. She was wrestling. You could see that this was an unanticipated moment for her—to offer a bit more transparency about the board's process. You could see her being compelled by her desire to be vulnerable and open with students while maintaining her responsibility to be measured as a board member. This wrestling was seen through long, pregnant pauses between her words, a verbal tug-of-war between saying more than what she may have planned and pulling back after sharing certain bits of information. She was walking a tightrope. Her sighs between sentences and breaks from her own train of thought to check in with students caused this town meeting to become something more than a scripted dialogue. As the meeting was concluding, faculty and students asked whether the community could talk a bit longer. A number of people left. She stayed.

A different moment of intimacy was possible between this board member and a group of students. I watched as this member stayed after the event, talking with various students about their anxieties and concerns. What caught my attention was the reactions of students to her. Their body language, such as proximity to her after the event and walking with her around the room as she engaged other students, communicated that they felt a sense of safety and belonging with her. They felt desired by her. So many institutional leaders desire the institution (to maintain its social status or financial wealth) in ways that leave students feeling outside the center of leaders' desires and practices of care. When every conversation feels as if the institution is privileging its bureaucratic affairs in ways that do not make clear student value and significance, a community of desire and belonging is lost. When students feel they are numbers on the utilitarian calculus of an institution's bottom line, caring and just community escapes us. I saw some students exchanging emails with this board member. This was something different from what I had witnessed before. A new moment was being made possible; burgeoning feelings of belonging were being forged—something we desperately need in hopes of being a different kind of community.

I am clear that this one exchange does not speak, in any way, to the larger structural dimensions of power and authority among boards and how people of color in theological institutions are often not served by the institutional decision making of such bodies. For certain, this town-hall scene of yearning and desire between this board member and students does not magically solve the dilemma of broken institutions and inequitable systems inside theological education. Instead, this moment is exemplary of how countercultural desires are born, through the breaking open of our hearts, minds, and bodies as we wrestle inside of surprising and unanticipated moments of intimacy, vulnerability, and transparency. These moments are unanticipated. Outside our control. Even unimagined. Yet, we find ourselves there, in them, experiencing new modes of relating to people we neither desire nor feel like we belong to. These are profound, significant moments that hold the power of reshaping who we are together. These moments of radical intimacy need not be pitted against the requirement of material and structural change. We need both.

I witnessed another moment of desire at this town-hall meeting. I was struck by a young white woman student who walked to the mic to address the community, particularly the board members and administration. She stated that as a Presbyterian student, she was willing for some of her academic funding (which is quite generous for Presbyterian students) to be cut and redistributed to black students, who disproportionately carry loads of debt after graduation. She asserted that her white privilege meant acknowledging the systemic ways in which she has benefited economically from Princeton's history of wealth creation, which has been on the backs of the enslaved. It wasn't so much what she said but how she said it that caught my attention. She said it as if this were a new moment for her, an awakening and realization of the racist nature of things. She was wrestling. She spoke with a slow cadence of conviction and with heartbreak in her eyes of the toll whiteness takes on everyone, including herself. I couldn't help but wonder if her statement felt like a rebirth for her, as a white student and as a future white ally.

The room was absolutely still, bone quiet; you could not even hear the breathing of the one hundred or so people in attendance. I curiously watched the facial expressions and body language of some white students, faculty, and administrators. Some of them were wrestling with such a sweeping pronouncement. For certain, those in the room, for the most part, supported some sort of reparations agenda. They were clear that previous and present African Americans experienced disenfranchisement at Princeton. Yet I could also see the power of this student's statement, of being in solidarity with black students in this way. Solidarity costs. Some white students were unclear if they could take this kind of risk; after all, debt after seminary life is a common experience, no matter one's racial affiliation. What does a statement like this truly mean for their own lives, when some of them are still barely surviving financially after graduation? Many white students understood the virtue of her statement, but they also live inside the financial distress and duress they experience after seminary. This statement produced anxiety and admiration, affirmation and fear, all at once. Is one not a white ally if one cannot live out this statement?

I was also hoping that her assertion would not be seen as merely performative—white allies making grand pronouncements that everyone knows could never be approved by the board or administration. I think her offer was genuine. I hoped that her statement would be seen as an invitation into a new kind of conversation about the courage, risk taking, and vulnerability necessary to inaugurate real intimacy and belonging in theological institutions in light of gross histories of racial pain and trauma. I also believe that her statement reminded white students and faculty that their role in addressing racial pain is costly, uncomfortable work. It is uncomfortable to talk about the financial, social, and institutional privileges that white people have in these spaces. It's even more shocking to rethink the sharing of these institutional resources and privileges with previously subjugated people, which means that one will have less institutional privilege to move in unilateral ways that ignore or dismiss the needs of racialized others. Building communities of intimacy and belonging happens through the work of the Spirit, but we participate in this work, through our courage, transparency, and willingness to risk our own comfort. We enable otherwise communities through counting the costs and following Jesus, as he reminded his disciples throughout the Gospels.

Some black students, through their actions, showed that they experienced her words as an invitation to create belonging. When she finished speaking, some black students immediately engaged her. Other black students needed time to process what was being said. Some black students were pulled into silent reflection after she spoke. After the event, a few black students told me how shocked they were to hear the young white woman student say this. One student, whom I will call Brian, admitted that he had had a hard time trusting white students at Princeton, and that this moment had created a real opening in his heart. He sought the woman out after the town hall, introduced himself, and talked to her. What if a new unlikely relationship was born?

What captivated me was the *desire* Brian felt for this white female student speaker. He remarked that he had a hard time trusting white people, which included white students here at Princeton Theological Seminary. His suspicions are certainly justified, given racist histories at Princeton and within the United States. This moment invited him into a new kind of desire to engage this white woman student. Similarly, I could tell that this white female student also felt the initiation of desire to be with and for black students on *their* terms. So many liberal conversations are halted because white interlocutors demand that the discussion of race and reparations be on their terms. Key words that are thrown out are "civility," "good will," and "solidarity." But these words do not really capture the risk and sacrifice white communities are called to embody as they discuss intersectional forms of structural racism. Such conversations involve entering into the worlds of black individuals who experience daily racist assault. The white female student's call to action was risky and showed that she understood the ethic of risk that should be part of any white community's desire to be allies. Brian was undone by this moment. It created intimacy between these two students. Such witnessing and risk taking are necessary to forge a new kind of community marked by trust and reciprocity.

I am not suggesting that this white woman saved the day. Instead, her act of naming the privilege from which she benefits and the risk she felt called to take opened up a new space. I heard other stories from white and black students at this town-hall meeting as well. They remarked that they began unlikely relationships because of these kinds of moments, where possibilities of intimacy and belonging emerged in ways that shocked and surprised. I am looking for these kinds of moments in theological education, moments that gesture toward an "otherwise economy" of desire than the one we have now in which students tolerate, fear, or put up with each other for the sake of a degree. We need to be undone by each other.

What if theological education could be experienced as a site where we might be undone by each other? Could this be more than a naïve question? Is being undone or experiencing the explosion of deep desire for another who previously felt alien possible? For a number of theologians and Christian leaders, the impulse is to reject this notion, insisting that it imagines profound transformation as an occurrence that happens simply within the self. I am aware of many accounts of Christian mystics and other saints who are undone by God's presence, an individual encounter that remakes and transforms the self. Although I find these accounts powerful, I am not referring to this notion of being undone. For others, being undone may have negative connotations. Being undone by someone might mean to be wounded and disoriented. I have talked about many instances in the academy where black women (such as myself) have felt wounded, completely robbed of affirmation and support. Being wounded is undesirable. It is the result of trauma and pain. Wounding is a deep reality, and theological institutions are experienced as sites of spiritual and moral injury. I am not denying that such injuries occur. But this description is not what I mean by being undone either.

For me, being undone is not simply about individual spiritual encounters with God. It requires others. Other bodies. Other narratives. Other stories. Different lives. Practices of witnessing. Mutual vulnerability that resists control. And inside of these fleshly encounters, something happens to *you*. In you, around you, through you. Being undone is a vulnerable space in which to reside as you lose control of your ability to dictate and determine the affective, felt encounter. Being undone requires a space where people are encountering each other face-to-face, where the substance of our different and sometimes conflicting lives collide, where one not only thinks about others but *feels* others on their own terms, where stories are being told that shock and surprise and pull us out of our fundamentalist presuppositions, where vulnerability is expressed through practices of witnessing. Being undone is risky. It invites new modes of being that refuse enmity having the last say. Being undone calls us to be witnesses.

Black feminist June Jordan reminds us that when we participate in witnessing, we are saying "nobody means more to me than you" in this moment.[1] We become vulnerable with and for another, and this "kind of vulnerability helps us constitute ourselves as agents in the world."[2] Witnessing is a practice that creates a space of vulnerability. However, we typically run from vulnerability. I understand why. In our society, vulnerability is exploited. It is weaponized against the vulnerable. As a result, being undone in a society that is marked by an instrumentalizing ethos is scary. For certain, the call for vulnerability must simultaneously acknowledge and dismantle exploitative power. But even after this, vulnerability is still risky. Despite the risks, what would it mean to embrace and not retreat from the possibility of our potential undoing?[3] This is what witnessing is about.

I am invested in schools of theological education becoming sites of witnessing. Witnessing can make a new social space possible. We need structural transformation, but we also need new social spaces where we can imagine creative communities characterized by healing and belonging. Black people (and people of color) want to witness to the multiple forms of violence to which they are subjected by social structures and practices within theological schools, churches, and broader society. This is important. To be able to witness is to name forms of violence other subjects cannot see or refuse to acknowledge.[4] But people also want to be able to witness to their yearnings and longings for hope. Hope in something different and new. To be able to witness is also to name forms of joy and world-making possibilities. We are not without hope.

* * *

Being undone and witnessing to another way of life involve hope. In my Pentecostal community, the enfleshed experience of the Spirit was about a communal awakening of desire connected to hope. During collective worship, it was not unusual to see people who had been having severe disagreements be pulled toward each other by a desire to begin again in their relationships. I certainly experienced this. In such moments, the spiritual "high" would impel me to go over to another member of the church at whom I'd been angry and, with tears streaming down my face, apologize and pledge to love that person better. Enmity often dissolved in these powerful collective moments. This experience of the Spirit transformed our desires for God and each other. After such an experience, we would eat Sunday lunch together and then come back that very night to experience it all again. We fought as much as we loved. We trusted that things could be different in light of our ongoing imperfections if only we could feel, touch, hear, and taste the Source in these moments of collective worship. We desired God and each other, but we also desired to be better than who we had been: more faithful, more loving, and more compassionate. To desire each other in our imperfections and to remain spiritually honest about our own level of complicity made these moments possible. It generated moments of being undone by each other and gave us strength to hope in the midst of potential resignation.

Our desires and visions of hope were driven by apocalyptic sensibilities, for sure. My community believed that Jesus was returning at any moment to judge the sinful and unholy. For a child, this is a terrifying idea. I recall as a child always wondering whether I had attained the needed level of spiritual transformation to be secure from eternal doom. We had to strive for moral perfection in the event that Jesus "broke through the clouds" to announce the coming judgment. This part of our theology never worked for me. I was constantly driven by fear in my spiritual life, and God was nothing more than an extreme taskmaster, ready to dispense wrath at any moment.

Yet an altogether unintended consequence of our apocalyptic sensibilities was the way in which it taught us to wait.

We lived our lives with longing and expectation. We expected a new way of being to unfold *within and beyond* the embattled present order in which we were situated. We saw powerful systems as thoroughly contingent, and therefore we never automatically granted them power. All social orders were fleeting and would pass away. The contingent character of institutions meant that new worlds could be born. In fact, a new world could be born as we waited, anticipated, and expected. In the meantime, we would allow our desires for God, each other, and the larger world to be shaped by what was to come.

Anything was possible in this world to come. In my tradition, miracles were commonplace—or at least the claim that miracles could happen was. A woman would come in with cancer, receive prayer, and one week later testify that the cancer had left her body. A man would enter the church in a wheelchair and, after receiving prayer from the church mothers and elders, get up and walk in front of the entire assembly. And when these miracles happened, the entire church community celebrated through dancing and shouting. Rationally, miracles do not make sense; they are not coherent or compatible with the physics of the universe. However, I cannot deny what I have seen with my own eyes: miracles happened, and they remain mysterious to me to this very day. This way of thinking about the world through a language of miracles is what marked my community. We abided in longings and yearnings for worlds that perhaps could not yet be seen but were already felt.

Pentecostal experience is an experience of yearning and longing for the reign of God now, but also for what is not yet. It is a yearning and longing at the level of body, of bodies waiting, eating, praying, living with, and loving each other. In my community, we waited together, desiring together. We hoped. We rejoiced in a future waiting to be born. In the midst of our imperfections and outright contradictions, we still desired to witness to newness of life.

I yearn for a new world to unfold and be born in theological education. My prayer is that theological education would be a context in which people will experience the transformation of their desires toward communities of intimacy and belonging in order to be witnesses. And this prayer is not merely about words. We must work. Our prayers must *be* our collective actions in fostering an otherwise future of care and trust. What might it look like to bear witness to other ways of being community? For white people who are leaders of theological institutions, they might begin truly to hear their native sons and daughters who experience forms of racist assault and work with them in transforming institutional structures. White students and faculty might acknowledge their hesitancies and discomfort in wrestling with their own white privilege (and how this often affects their relationships with students and faculty of color) and engage their brothers and sisters of color to offer a sense of belonging and ongoing friendship. Faculty and students of color might ask if they are open to entering potentially new moments of intimacy and belonging with (primarily) white others who seek accountability and wrestle inside of these moments instead of immediately self-protecting. Another future involves bearing witness to what is possible, but this requires all parties stretching toward different ways of being. We must hope together, pray together, and then act in ways that reflect just, compassionate relations.

* * *

We can be witnesses to new worlds through a commitment to being prophetic. In liberal theological institutions, we talk about "the prophetic" quite a bit, but what does this mean? Christian liberals often speak of "prophetic witness" while continuing to inhabit moderate or even regressive positions. When I speak of the prophetic, I am talking about people who embody transgressive ways of resisting death-dealing powers, practices, and desires that might make them marginal or unpopular. In progressive Christian circles today, the idea of the prophetic is treated as a badge of political correctness. It is seen as a gig that might enable one to gain popularity and celebrity status. One need only post messages on Facebook about Jesus and social justice to appear to be prophetic (or at least part of the Christian liberal in-group). Being prophetic is often treated as a form of social capital to advance one's own naked ambitions. Being prophetic has tremendous currency on the liberal religious and political stage, at times making prophetic voices nothing more than an aspect of political theater.

When I speak of the prophetic, I mean something altogether different. Being prophetic is about moral courage. Being prophetic is about risking oneself for the sake of others. For instance, I have written extensively about the black church's political agency in engaging structural racism. It is often assumed that all black clergy leaders were in solidarity with Martin Luther King Jr., marching and protesting the demonic systems of racial segregation and apartheid. But this is a nostalgic interpretation, an idealistic way of looking back on black history. Very few black clergy leaders were in solidarity with King's methods of nonviolent resistance at the height of the marches and direct protests. Many black leaders felt that such methods were dangerous and unwise, and could make one a target of police or white vigilante retribution. Moreover, many black parents at the time felt that King was a propagandist taking advantage of the fact that the majority of bodies on the front lines of the civil rights movement were youth. Under Ella Baker's leadership and mentorship, the Student Nonviolent Coordinating Committee (SNCC) mobilized thousands of college students around the nation to participate in the marches and protests. Their parents were not always supportive.

Participating in these forms of resistance could cost a person her or his life. When civil rights leaders such as King led risky protests, they found themselves alienated and exiled. We are familiar with how King's own organization alienated him after he spoke out against the Vietnam War. Perhaps we are less familiar with the reality that public opinion turned against him, too. White politicians *and* black religious leaders (such as the Southern Christian Leadership Conference [SCLC] organization he led) asked why he would incite rebellion when the civil rights movement had gained so much traction in overturning antidiscrimination laws in housing, education, and employment? For King, being prophetic meant enduring the pain and even trauma of going against majority public opinion. Being prophetic is about the embodiment of moral courage, which is an unpleasant, uncomfortable, and often lonely position to occupy.

Being prophetic also involves the transformation of our desires. Beyond King, many black prophetic voices envisioned new economies of desire. Bayard Rustin is one example. Rustin was central to King's embrace of nonviolent resistance and civil disobedience as spiritual practices *first*. Prior to engaging Rustin, King had not been persuaded of the efficacy of nonviolent resistance. It was Rustin who shaped King's devotion to methods of nonviolence as a spiritual and not merely a political practice. As a black Quaker, Rustin was formed by a different economy of desire birthed through nonviolent resistance. Rustin embraced the philosophy of nonviolence that Quaker faith espoused (although this faith has its own history of internal racial violence). For Rustin, nonviolent resistance made the ground ready for the potential transformation of desires among friends and enemies. Nonviolent resistance was about the *force of truth* in unmasking an economy of alienation and separation built on bitter racial hatred. Whites experienced the malformation of their own humanity when the racial order did not allow whites to connect and commune with black people *affectively*. Similarly, black communities lived in fear and resentment of white racial hatred and systemic harm, which understandably made many blacks reject the possibility of real community with whites. An economy built on disgust, resentment, and fear plagued and continues to afflict American society and American churches. Rustin wanted King and the civil rights movement to embrace nonviolent resistance in order to gesture toward a new economy of desire.

Rustin wanted to envision *otherwise* desires that moved beyond fear and resentment. He knew that we are more than our resentments. That would not be easy for Rustin. Rustin was at the forefront of organizing the March on Washington, as he had considerable experience and expertise in grassroots organizing and was esteemed for it. However, when Rustin came out as a black gay man, leaders within the civil rights movement distanced themselves from him and urged King abruptly to end his camaraderie and organizing relationship with Rustin. Exiled both from broader white society and from his own black community, Rustin, as a black and gay man, was clear that to be open about his sexuality in efforts to support other sexually different persons would come at a cost. It was a cost he did not shirk. Rustin was rejected because of affective economies of disgust that prevented SCLC leaders from opting to experience deep solidarity with him in order to bear witness to a different kind of community, one marked by more radical inclusion.

Rustin is one of many black persons who embodied prophetic witness by attempting to change malformed economies of desire. Lorraine Hansberry is another. Through her literary work, she imagined a new economy of desire away from the capitalist gaze. I have already talked about her impact on my intellectual journey as a young black woman. When Hansberry's *Raisin in the Sun* was reviewed, it was met with approval and praise. White mainstream America hailed it as a story about the American Dream and the struggle a black family had in securing this dream. Although this made Hansberry uncomfortable (as it was more truly and broadly a play about race in America and how black people were deeply affected by capitalist desires), she nevertheless experienced the critics' celebration and support.

However, that was not always to be the case. She put herself on the line to speak transparently about racial segregation, especially regarding the masses of poor blacks who were trapped in an American system of racial apartheid. Consider how black scholar Imani Perry writes about an encounter between Hansberry and Robert Kennedy, who served as attorney general under President John Kennedy. The attorney general invited Hansberry, along with prominent black artists and celebrities, to meet with him to discuss the problem of segregation and racism in the country. In particular, the attorney general wanted to figure out how black leaders could help quell the confrontations between black communities and white Southern police, encounters that often resulted in violence. In the middle of this meeting, Jerome Smith, an organizer of the Southern freedom movement, asked whether the government would take real steps in protecting the civil rights of African Americans. Jerome had personally faced gun violence and beatings with no protection from the federal government. James Baldwin recalled that Robert Kennedy turned away from Jerome as if to indicate that he was not an important or desirable voice in the room. Kennedy felt that Smith was too aggressive and angry. Kennedy's apparent immediate dismissal of Smith's rage was driven by Kennedy's assumption that Smith reflected a kind of uncivilized anger that Kennedy had no intention of engaging. Smith was not the kind of respectable black leader that Kennedy desired as a conversation partner.[5]

Perry recounts how Hansberry responded. Hansberry turned to the attorney general and stated that the only voice to which he should be listening was the voice of Smith, who had directly experienced state violence. Indeed, said Hansberry, Smith's voice was the voice of twenty-two million people affected by state brutality under the Jim Crow system. After having had her say, she turned around and walked out.[6] She would not be seduced by having access to power, a common strategy white power structures use to keep black leaders silent. In that moment, she did not desire white approval or social capital. When Hansberry responded in this way, Kennedy sat and stared in disbelief at her unwillingness to be "moderate" and compromise. He didn't understand why she was rejecting what was often desirable to black leaders: proximity to white institutional power. Hansberry was not invited back. Robert Kennedy considered the meeting a tremendous waste of time.[7]

Hansberry's prophetic witness teaches us about an alternative economy of desire. She did not want to mimic malformed desires of black respectability despite her own celebrated status. For her, it was not enough to be celebrated. She could not relish her own success when it meant the continued disenfranchisement of the black masses. She wanted to bear witness to an American society that *desired* to listen to the "Jeromes" of the world. The problem was that white religious and political leaders did not desire communities marked by justice, care, and compassion *because they did not desire Jerome Smith.* They wanted to grant the bare minimum in order to preserve the established political order in which elite whites had the power. A transformation of desire was necessary to understand why ignoring the Jeromes of our country undermined the entire democratic project. In part, I imagine that this is what Lorraine Hansberry wanted to communicate.

Like Rustin and Hansberry, I have learned that being prophetic costs something. It makes me a target. It often results in me feeling unpopular and misunderstood. I know others who feel this way. Yet I cannot ignore the payoff: being prophetic can transform problematic economies of desire. We need a model of theological education that truly embodies the prophetic.

* * *

Social movements are providing contexts wherein people can be witnesses to otherwise economies of desire. What would it mean for theological education to listen more deeply to these movements in order to offer spaces that are more just and welcoming for native daughters and sons?

The twenty-first century has given us public social movements that have incarnated what it means to be prophetic and to imagine alternative economies of desire, new movements that announce otherwise longings, yearnings, and energies for different ways of being community. Many people that have been part of social movements have been Christian leaders of faith. We often think that Christian leaders come fully formed to social movements. We often imagine that our ATS-accredited seminaries and divinity schools as well as Bible institutes have a monopoly on theological formation. But that is not always the case.

Social movements have *incubated* faith leaders and transformed their desires in relation to questions of belonging and inclusion. Individuals are experiencing leadership formation in other contexts such as public movements that move into the streets. Countless black and white clergypersons have been transformed by participating in protests associated with Black Lives Matter. Many faith leaders have remarked that their idea of who and what the church truly is underwent a profound shift thanks to these protests. The church is not merely those who gather in a building to hear the preached Word and receive the sacraments; it is those who *show up as Christ's body*, who demonstrate unconditional love to those under the heel of distorted institutional power, who stand in solidarity with those who are dispossessed and in need of salvation from sinful structures of oppression. *Being* Christ in the world means desiring the other, the marginal person, the one who is left out of society. Being the church is about living into the gospel in deed, through action—a desire that finds its fulfillment in my neighbor, no matter how different that neighbor is from myself. Anecdotally, some faith leaders I know personally asserted that they actually *became Christian* through engaging this prophetic social movement. They were formed in a way that helped them to discern how to be the presence of Christ on the earth. These leaders saw Christian practice *as* public social movement marked by the joining together of lives.

Over the last several decades, theological education has not been completely deaf to social movements. From the 1950s to the 1990s, theological schools recognized their contributions. A number of theological scholars certainly reflected on the importance of various public movements in rethinking Christian witness and practice within this country. Feminist theologians such as Rosemary Radford Ruether and Sharon Welch brought insights from the women's liberation movement into theological schools. These feminist thinkers reflected on patriarchal language about God as well as ecclesial policies that excluded women from ordination and other religious offices. Various black theologians, such as James Cone and J. Deotis Roberts, employed the insights of the black power movement to rethink Jesus's "blackness" as being his solidarity with and among the oppressed and vulnerable within society. Black women theologians and ethicists such as Jacquelyn Grant, Katie Cannon, and Traci West created womanist and black feminist theological discourses in light of black women's experiences and activism, which drew attention to questions of intersectionality. Queer theologians such as Horace Griffin and Renee Hill reflected on the problems of fixed notions of gender and sexuality, which barred nonheteronormative people from being a full part of churches. These movements had real effects on individual theologians and how they critiqued and reconstructed theological discourses.

Yet, theological institutions have never had a sustained conversation on how these rich theological discourses informed by social movements reshape institutional economies of desire—how they transform what is valued and centered within theological education. For instance, only in the last five to ten years have a number of seminaries and divinity schools awarded tenure to their first African American scholar or person of color. Some theological institutions are just inaugurating their "firsts" in various areas. I know that I am the first black woman to be hired in Princeton Theological Seminary's theology department, but not because there have not been black women theologians and theological ethicists to hire over the past several decades. This is a hard truth. It is difficult for theological institutions to admit that they have treated theological scholars of color badly and as marginal. Some institutions treat scholars of color as absentees within their institutional culture.

On arriving at Princeton, I was aware of a deep concern among many LGBTQ students there: They did not feel they were desired. They did not feel they belonged. The second year I was at Princeton, a series of events shook our community. Most shocking was a homophobic letter sent from an anonymous email account to the BGLASS (Bisexual, Gay, Lesbian, and Straight Supporters) group. The letter condemned same-gender-loving students. The letter dripped with anger, hate, and intolerance. Many BGLASS students felt violated and unsafe in an institutional context that had been trying to do the work of institutional inclusion. This event resurfaced old wounds and made healing and dialogue a more distant reality.

As an institution, we responded with a series of conversations. The theology department specifically responded by establishing a queer theology course, our first theology course on same-gender studies. Various professors had taught texts on queer theology within their respective courses, but the decision to dedicate an entire course to queer theology indicated a shift in the institution's theological sensibilities. It communicated that theology cannot be done without substantive reflection on how queer theology transforms theological categories and Christian practices altogether. Queer thought offers a reenvisioning of what it means to be a Christian, especially in a conservative Christian milieu where being gay and Christian is seen as incompatible and even antagonistic. I recognize that our response at the seminary was precisely that: only a response. Indeed, the vast majority of theological schools simply respond to particular events or situations that involve harm and trauma among same-gender-loving persons. What might happen if theological institutions *proactively* made decisions about LGBTQ belonging as part of a radical vision of inclusion rather than making these kinds of decisions from a *reactive* posture?

Yet, being proactive in *this way* is often eclipsed by locating the seeds of radical change in curricular reform. When most theological schools speak of institutional transformation, they focus predominantly on changes in curriculum and pedagogy. Certainly curriculum matters in how we think about knowledge and practice. Including diverse discourses, particularly topics and ideas that represent marginalized and oppressed narratives of the world, is indispensable to casting a radical vision of theological education. I am clear that when black, Latinx, and Asian discourses are not part of introductory courses in biblical studies, theology, ethics, history of Christianity, and more, something is lost. It is easy to ghettoize black theological sources to homiletics and practical theology (although all theology is practical, in my estimation). Courses that do not foreground classical European sources and texts ought not to be relegated to electives. They need to be part of the core curriculum. Moreover, when pedagogical practices privilege one primary way of learning, students are left behind. Students come to seminary with diverse learning styles, some from oral cultures like my own. Yet, they are colonized to a European-rooted model of paper writing in which the only form of learning that counts is the kind that can be structured into a very particular sort of argument. There are merits to knowing how to write such an argument. But there are other forms of knowledge and learning that demonstrate skill and proficiency, such as oral presentations that offer a compelling vision of a particular matter, collaborative projects among students that allow a collective search for knowledge, and field or community engagement that allows one to test ideas out in the broader world. These additional forms of teaching and learning allow students with multiple backgrounds to access the learning moment, asking how the material they learn illuminates the worlds from which they come and to and with which they will return and engage. Being aware of the need for a more expansive pedagogical practice does remain central to articulating a radical vision of theological education where leaders are formed to engage the world effectively.

Yet these observations I am making about curriculum and pedagogy are often seen as what makes a theological vision of education radical. But is the curriculum the primary site of radical revolution in relation to theological education? Should it be? While not denying the importance of curriculum revision, I do want to challenge our proclivity to depend on curriculum reform as the primary agent of transformation in theological education. We tend to be certain about what curriculum changes are needed and what revisions to it will yield. We are less attentive to other major institutional dimensions that *must* change if theological institutions are to be released to a different, more liberative future. Our economies of desire must be transformed. Curriculum doesn't answer this problem fully. Curriculum is one aspect, but there are many other aspects that prepare the ground for sweeping transformations in theological education.

* * *

I am hesitant to offer a defined program of transformative theological education. Every context is different and requires specific energies, commitments, and actions. Nonetheless, I do want to offer some concluding meditations on how otherwise economies of desire might transform practices of formation and leadership.

Alternative economies of desire might lead to new visions of formation. I think different yearnings and energies drive *why* students attend theological institutions today. More seminary students are becoming clear that they want to use their degree in service to faith activism and advocacy that are not dependent on ecclesial institutions and church politics. They want to build communities that are *otherwise*, that is, *other than* what is present. While I was doing my master's in religion, one of my student colleagues was interested in political practices of faith that were not necessarily connected with institutional church structures at all. My colleague was a former lawyer who envisioned working with a not-for-profit that sought to educate faith-based leaders and organizations on how to impact the larger public square. Again, the emphasis of this work did not privilege churches as the center of advocacy work. Churches were one center among many organizational centers. Many students' vocational paths represent a departure from the traditional purposes and end goals of theological education—the assumption that this education is primarily in preparation for full-time, ordained leadership of a congregation.

Students who attend seminaries and divinity schools may have vocational desires that do not align with traditional goals of ministry, but they nevertheless have something to teach us about theological education. These students do not see themselves as training to be institutional leaders at all within churches. These nontraditional students come with the explicit purpose of contributing to humanitarian or social justice projects that are not always connected to organized religious communities. Having taught at Brite Divinity School and now at Princeton, I always had a substantial number of students that enrolled in divinity school or seminary for reasons other than to prepare for ordination or an academic career. Take the community organizer who is a "follower of Jesus" but not in the traditional sense of being doctrinal or connected to the church. She attends seminary to understand better what motivates people of faith to organize in hopes of collaborating with religious communities in the work for justice. She doesn't attend seminary in order to maintain orthodox theology or institutional church commitments. In fact, she unapologetically disagrees with much of organized Christianity. But she does recognize that Christians have strong theological reasons for pursuing social justice, and she wants to delve deeply into these accounts of Christian faith. The point for this community organizer *is not to preserve the church. Rather, it's to understand the people who constitute Christian churches.* Students like her come to seminary not necessarily to defend or preserve church doctrines or structures but to understand and engage these structures better as faith-filled persons.

Moreover, the community organizer might have an interest in broader interreligious engagement. This organizer may genuinely want to enter into interreligious dialogue on how to live well together in the midst of real differences within society. In a culture that is painfully fragmented across social and religious divides, these kinds of students see their desire to enroll in divinity school as an act of good faith. They wish to shape new practices of religious understanding that can quell ongoing violence within public spaces due to fear, hatred, and misunderstanding. Their motivation for coming to seminary is profoundly different from that of students in the past, who typically centered the church as the primary form of hope within the world. The community organizer would not deny that the church is one possible agent of hope. But she would add that it is one among many such communities that are thinking hopefully about a more tolerant, loving, and just future.

Numerous students entering divinity schools and seminaries have no desire to train for institutional church leadership (at any level), but they are still people of faith, leaders of faith. Their focus may not be the church, but their emphasis is certainly on how forms of Christian spirituality can transform broader society. These students of faith are less concerned with how their agency is made possible in and through institutional church settings and structures and more concerned with how their own burgeoning personal understandings of faith create new openings for Christian witness and social change.

Seminary institutions that see perpetuation of the institutional church as their *raison d'être* may view these students with suspicion. Not me. I am interested in how these students participate in alternative economies of desire that yearn and long for people across multiple differences—racial, class, *and* religious differences. This yearning to come into community with people that the church historically has identified as outliers, heretics, or threats announces a different kind of desire. It is the desire for the multitude, a longing for all nations and cultures, all those Jesus gathered and engaged without requirements, without assent to orthodoxy or creeds. These students desire to participate in a theology of joining that moves across multiple barriers, even religious barriers.

I am not suggesting that we leave churches behind. I am deeply committed to who and what churches are called to be. Instead, I am suggesting that we might learn quite a bit from students who are located outside the bounds of organized Christianity. At least at Princeton Theological Seminary, I am asking us to look at the countercultural desires for the other that these unorthodox students often possess—a desire I tend to find lacking in church-oriented students whose primary understanding of Christian identity involves, at times, policing doctrinal boundaries. I am attracted to how these unorthodox students are open to being "undone" by others. I am interested in how their sense of formation, the kind of humility they exercise, allows for unanticipated moments of intimacy and belonging across real differences. Leaders of theological education might meditate on this reality.

I am looking for a way for us to become undone by each other. To truly believe in an *otherwise* way of being human within the context of theological education. In the form of a prayer, my desire to become undone by others is not to deny the important work of systemic change in response to structural racism in theological education. I have dedicated most of my book to this specific discussion. But I also want to hold on to the belief that we can *begin again*—we can hope for diverse, truth-telling, and healing communities that defy how we presently exist. Without this, we are lost.

Postscript

I am finishing these notes in the middle of the coronavirus pandemic. Theological education, as many of us know it, has come to a halt. We are living in different times. We feel this palpably, as schools have decided to offer all or most of their classes online and professors have had to rethink strategies of community and connection. What does it mean to be a witness in this moment? For me, this coronavirus pandemic moves front and center what has always been present: deep disparities between the well-to-do and the rest of the country. This crisis continues to uncover a tale of two Americas. In one America, professional classes have had the luxury of staying home and doing work from home, drawing a paycheck despite the social, political, and economic chaos caused by the pandemic. The other America is populated by persons that are attempting to survive. They are labeled the "essential workers" of this pandemic, although they barely get paid a minimum wage. This other America disproportionately contains people of color and the economically disadvantaged more broadly.

Even more alarming, I find myself lamenting over the real fears of native daughters and sons in this moment. Their fears are not just about the virus itself. They have real fears about how they will navigate within the white academic context of theological education given the direct impact of this virus on their families and communities. I have a student who is from New York

City, and more specifically a borough that was hit the hardest, revealing disproportionate death among blacks and Latinx. She contacted me after losing one relative and having another relative in critical condition. I will never forget what the student asked me when making contact: "I don't think I can finish the semester, and I need to defer my assignments. But I don't want to be seen as a problem. How do I avoid this?" What immediately arrested my attention was not her request to defer assignments. I was shocked by her real question: *How can I not be seen as a problem?* What does it mean when native daughters (and sons) feel this pressure, this sense of being a problem, of trying to come to terms with feeling potentially misunderstood in white spaces of theological education? This fear about being a problem is not actually about whether *some* white people see them as a threat or not. This is not the point. Rather, native daughters and sons are affected by an entire set of historical and contemporary experiences of structural racism, which shapes their sense of belonging within white spaces. This student registered a tension: she certainly felt good about the rich resources and learning context of Princeton Seminary, but she equally felt that this context could easily interpret her as a problem. These are the tensions, the contradictions, the insider/outsider dynamics that mark native daughters and sons in much of theological education.

This feeling among native daughters and sons of being seen as a problem is deeply connected to the racial duress experienced within broader society. In the middle of this pandemic, we are also witnessing global uprisings over the thoughtless dehumanization and murder of black lives. In US cities and other places around the world (London, Hong Kong, etc.), people across racial communities have joined in decrying how black lives are treated as disposable and marginal. Widespread, unprecedented protests surrounding the police murders of Breonna Taylor and George Floyd demonstrated that black communities were no longer going to accept senseless killings justified by American law. People protested how American policing creates contexts of modern-day lynchings for blacks. American citizens continue to challenge how whiteness perpetually sets the terms of black disenfranchisement in education, criminal justice, employment, and more. In 2020, we found ourselves living through a different moment in which people across racial affiliations joined black communities in lifting up the need to protect black lives in this country. This was surprising and unexpected. Moments of intimacy and belonging certainly transpired at these protests and reminded me that we are only as strong as the relationships we build in the pursuit of justice work.

Even more shocking, we began witnessing unprecedented responses by governmental officials. I was surprised when the Minneapolis city council approved a proposal to defund the police and to redirect millions of dollars toward other community-building projects that could ensure a more holistic program for public safety, violence prevention, and communal well-being. This felt radical to me, as if local leaders were finally grasping the kinds of physical and social deaths that black communities wrestle down in order to survive and thrive. Even though defunding efforts in Minneapolis have not gotten very far to date, seeing the defunding of the police as a *possibility* moves in the direction of justice. We also watched as the perennial debate over whether national symbols rooted in slavery and segregation should be taken down or allowed to remain. I personally rejoiced when I watched Mississippi quietly take down its state flag marked by a Confederate symbol, which continues to cause deep pain among blacks in that state. Even at Princeton University, officials announced that they would be changing the name of the Woodrow Wilson School of Public Policy because of Wilson's racist policies and practices. Some argued against these measures by positing that these symbols and monuments allow us to face the ugly history of America and address it, instead of erasing it from our national sites. But I wonder: Do I need to be reminded through monuments and symbols of the insidious history of racial apartheid in order to grasp how corrupting and distorting American racism has been? What if we just told the truth about our racist history through how we taught American history in primary and

secondary schools of education? What if we introduced reparations to atone and repair parts of America's brutal antiblack
history? What if we wrestled, as a nation, with whiteness as the
foundation that makes possible structural racism? It seems
harder to invest in *these* kinds of measures. So many argue to
preserve these symbols of hate, touting them as needed for cultural preservation or important to the telling of American history.
What I realize is that perhaps we are living through a rewriting
of history that highlights the stories and voices of those crushed
underneath American empire. Perhaps this moment might allow
America to start again in envisioning a more just world free of the
original sin of racism.

We are living through a rewriting of history. The question is:
Will theological education take these same risks? Will it tear
down its own idols and monuments dedicated to ongoing whiteness and structural racism? Will theological education acknowledge that movements for truth telling and justice within its own
enterprise are upon us? Will theological education respond to
the times and alter its course? Some theological institutions are
rising to the challenge of this moment. Others, deep down, are
holding on and lamenting the loss of old ways, hierarchies, and
modes of educational life. I am looking for theological institutions that will bravely walk into this rapidly changing moment,
into the unknown, and desire truth telling and justice. I hope
that native daughters and sons can be part of envisioning what
this otherwise, just world might look like.

As a professor, I want to witness to an otherwise moment of
welcoming native daughters and sons; of wrestling down and
substantively engaging white anxiety and privilege over issues
of structural racism; of asking how our practices of intimacy and
belonging in theological education can be truly inclusive and
radical; of believing that hope in justice and healing are equally
important in order to experience the kind of beloved communities we need to make the future of theological education truly
liberating. I want my black students to *feel* another set of emotional possibilities when engaging our theological communities.

I want our theological institutions not to settle for institutional preservation but courageously to lead communities into futures of love, care, and justice. But this is possible only when we are open to otherwise moments that acknowledge and name racial trauma and pain, moments that shock us with unanticipated experiences of intimacy because we have been truthful and vulnerable, moments that cultivate spaces for institutional accountability and transparency, moments that teach us something about communities of belonging.

So I testify and I hope. I testify to the complexities and contradictions of the past and present of theological education. I testify to what has been lost as well as what has been gained. And I testify to what futures might be on the horizon. I hope for otherwise desires—as a form of prayer and action. I hope desperately for us to experience new economies of desire, connection, and belonging. The future of theological education depends on this.

For Further Thought

(Five Invitations for Further Reading, Community Conversation, and Action)

1. Read Jennifer Harvey. *Dear White Christians: For Those Still Longing for Racial Reconciliation.* Grand Rapids: Eerdmans, 2014.

    Invitation: Do a school-wide reading of this text and hold two or three community conversations among students, faculty, administrators, and staff about problems and responses to structural racism that native daughters and sons experience within *your* institution. How does Harvey's book directly challenge your institutional context of whiteness?

2. Read Yvette Flunder. *Where the Edge Gathers: Building a Community of Radical Inclusion.* Cleveland: Pilgrim, 2005.

    Invitation: Ponder with a small group of diverse students and faculty this collection of sermons/essays and how they help leaders attend to and gather those who are ignored and silenced.

3. Read *Princeton Seminary and Slavery: A Report of the Historical Audit Committee.* https://slavery.ptsem.edu/.

    Invitation: Have a school-wide conversation about this audit and the question of reparations. What kind of shift is necessary in *your* school to hear and respond to native daughters and sons? Might your institution conduct a slavery audit? If so, what would be some first steps?

4. Read Nancy Lynne Westfield. *Being Black, Teaching Black: Politics and Pedagogy in Religious Studies.* Nashville: Abingdon, 2008.

    Invitation: Institutionally support black faculty and PhD students gathering for times of group fellowship to discuss the racial politics of the academy, to share personal experiences, and to strategize ways forward within theological education that honors the scholarly gifts, pedagogical commitments, and structural needs of black faculty and students.

5. Read Leah Gunning Frances. *Ferguson and Faith: Sparking Leadership and Awakening Community.* St. Louis: Chalice, 2015.

    Invitation: Set up semester- or yearlong conversations with community activists and movement builders on questions of racial, gender, sexual, and class injustices. How might your institution form leaders within theological education differently when engaging social movements?

Notes

Introduction

1. For documentation for this paragraph, see Frank Yamada, "Living and Teaching When Change Is the New Normal: Trends in Theological Education and the Impact on Teaching and Learning," *Wabash Center Journal on Teaching* 1, no. 1 (2020): 23–36; see especially 31–32.

Chapter 1

1. Willie Jennings, *Acts: A Theological Commentary on the Bible* (Louisville: Westminster John Knox, 2017), 27.

2. Jennings, *Acts*, 27.

3. See Michael Johnson's editing of Lincoln's speeches and essays on a wide range of issues such as free labor, slavery, and secession, plus the Civil War, emancipation, and more in *Abraham Lincoln, Slavery, and the Civil War: Selected Writings and Speeches* (Boston: Bedford/St. Martin's, 2011). This text reveals Lincoln as a pragmatist who understood his political positions broadly as pragmatic moves in the interests of American capitalism and political community. Lincoln was less a moralist on the question of slavery than a *pragmatist*. Lincoln himself states that he would have left slavery intact had it preserved the Union. While Lincoln did not see slavery as a natural condition to be desired, he was not driven solely by the moral argument against slavery. For him, it was chiefly a question of *economics*, how the country needed to move forward in light of the Industrial Revolution transpiring in the North. As a pragmatist, he recognized that America was at a critical

moment and needed to secure its economic and political future in the face of European competition. While this pragmatic perspective of Lincoln is less romantic, it does offer a realistic and complex portrait of a man who navigated the tricky matrices of racial hegemony in the United States. Like Lincoln, Springfield also possesses this paradox. As I entered my teenage years, I began to realize that the myth of Lincoln presented a larger problem in the self-understanding of my hometown.

4. Craig Steven Wilder, *Ebony and Ivy: Race, Slavery and the Troubled History of America's Universities* (London: Bloomsbury, 2014), 113–14.

5. Mattie Moss Clark, "No Escape and No Excuse" (sermon delivered at 1983 Church of God in Christ Women's Convention in Miami, Florida, published online April 16, 2018), https://www.youtube.com/watch?v=flWHG4E-dGE.

6. Zora Neale Hurston, *The Sanctified Church: The Folklore Writings of Zora Neale Hurston* (Berkeley, CA: Turtle Island Foundation, 1983). See p. 59 where she writes, "The self-despisement lies in a middle class who scorns to do or be anything Negro . . . he [middle-class Negro] wears drab clothing, sits through a boresome church service, pretends to have no interest in the community, holds beauty contests, and otherwise apes all the mediocrities of the white brother."

7. See Hurston, *The Sanctified Church*, 83, where Hurston discusses how individual members in Pentecostal worship services are allowed to "hang new ornaments" on the tradition, which gestures toward the creative and artistic view of Pentecostal life. For Hurston, this kind of religious expression is not irrational and emotive but "art."

8. I recognize that not every scholar of homiletics likes the language of "exegeting the congregation." James Nieman objects to it because he considers a congregation not a text to be read, a thing to be objectified and manipulated. Instead, he maintains that a congregation has a context that must be interpreted and understood. I agree with Nieman that such a metaphor can lead to such objectification. However, the exegesis metaphor does address the ways in which both language and practices structure the worldviews and webs of significance of religious communities as well as our need to understand these linguistic maps and fleshly practices to interpret a community's self-understanding accurately.

9. Clifford Geertz, *Interpretation of Cultures* (New York: Basic Books, 1977). Refer to chapter 4, "Religion as a Cultural System," and pp. 89–95 where Geertz discusses how humans are "suspended in webs of significance" that humans themselves have spun. Because any culture is made up of these webs of significance, any analysis of this culture is based not on scientific laws but on interpretative approaches in search of meaning.

10. Nora Tisdale, *Preaching as Local Theology and Folk Art* (Minneapolis: Fortress, 1997). Refer to p. 89, where she employs the metaphor of a "storied mirror" in discussing how one interprets congregations and their broader religious life.

Chapter 2

1. The Association of Theological Schools (ATS) is an accrediting organization that maintains and evaluates academic standards related to theological education. The ATS also has a history of providing diversity reports in theological education. My argument here is not that ATS does not focus on issues of diversity. Rather, I am pointing out that ATS has not done an official report that documents structural racism in theological institutions. It seems to me that this is needed, whether ATS undertakes this report itself or funds an organization to provide some kind of comprehensive reporting in this area.

2. James Moorhead, *Princeton Seminary in American Religion and Culture* (Grand Rapids: Eerdmans, 2012), 12.

3. Moorhead, *Princeton Seminary*, 14.

4. Moorhead, *Princeton Seminary*, 16.

5. See James Moorhead, "Princeton Theological Seminary and Slavery Report," *Princeton and Slavery Project*, accessed September 11, 2020, https://slavery.princeton.edu/stories/princeton-theological-seminary-and-slavery #3355; see under heading "Slave-Owning Faculty."

6. See Linda Darling-Hammond, "Unequal Opportunity: Race and Education," *Brookings*, March 1, 1998, https://www.brookings.edu/articles/unequal -opportunity-race-and-education/. In current discussions, universities are grappling with their links to slavery and racism and the lingering effect racism has on college life. One example would be Princeton University, which funded an entire conference about their historical findings and ongoing strategies to combat institutional racism at the school. See their website for more information: https://slavery.princeton.edu/.

7. Stephanie Buckhanon Crowder, "To Be Unaccepted," *Inside Higher Ed*, March 24, 2015, https://www.insidehighered.com/advice/2015/03/24/essay -being-denied-tenure.

8. Anemona Hartocollis, "A New Battleground over Political Correctness: Duke Divinity School," *New York Times*, May 9, 2017, https://www.nytimes .com/2017/05/09/education/a-new-battleground-over-political-correctness -duke-divinity-school.html.

9. Colleen Flaherty, "More Faculty Diversity, Not on Tenure Track," *Inside Higher Ed*, August 22, 2016, https://www.insidehighered.com/news/2016/08/22/study-finds-gains-faculty-diversity-not-tenure-track.

10. Nick Chiles, "Black Ministry Students at Duke Say They Face Unequal Treatment and Racism," NPR, May 24, 2017, http://www.npr.org/sections/codeswitch/2017/05/24/467233031/black-ministry-students-at-duke-say-they-face-unequal-treatment-and-racism.

11. Chiles, "Black Ministry Students at Duke Say They Face Unequal Treatment and Racism."

12. Monica Coleman, "Must I Be a Womanist?," *Journal of Feminist Studies in Religion* 22, no. 1 (Spring 2006): 85–96.

Chapter 3

1. Please refer to Lorraine Hansberry's *To Be Young, Gifted and Black*, illustrated ed. (New York: Signet, 2011), a collection of her writings that reveal her inner thoughts, desires, and aspirations. There is an uncanny resemblance between Lorraine's coming-of-age story and the character Beneatha.

2. Miles Jones, "Why a Black Seminary?," *Christian Century*, February 1972, 124.

3. Jones, "Why a Black Seminary?," 132. I also infer from Jones that the gift of black educational schools is in how they use black experience as a source for describing divine and social realities, which aids in black people's own liberation from white racist structures. The compelling aspect of Jones's argument is his assertion that black people must be given the freedom to trust their own voices and experiences in their educational formation processes, which include theological formation. I think that Jones's centering of black experience is not naïve, as he is well aware of the extremities of experience and how black communities have navigated such complexities in describing central truths about ultimate reality (being God and God's activity in the world). For me, Jones makes his point well: black seminaries resist totalizing interpretations of Christian experience and identity that often mark white seminaries, totalizing interpretations that often form the bedrock of theological education in the United States.

4. Delores Williams, "One Black Woman Reflects on Union," *Union Dues* 2, no. 1 (November 8, 1978): 4.

5. Katie Cannon, "Metalogues and Dialogues: Teaching the Womanist Idea," *Journal of Feminist Studies in Religion* 8, no. 2 (Fall 1992): 126.

6. Cannon, "Metalogues and Dialogues," 130.

7. Cannon, "Metalogues and Dialogues," 130.

8. Cecil Robeck, *The Azusa Street Mission and Revival: The Birth of the Global Pentecostal Movement* (Nashville: Nelson, 2017), 55.

9. Iain MacRobert, *The Black Roots and White Racism of Early Pentecostalism in USA* (London: Palgrave Macmillan, 1988), 56.

10. Yvette Flunder, *Where the Edge Gathers: Building a Community of Radical Inclusion* (Cleveland: Pilgrim, 2005), x.

Chapter 4

1. June Jordan, cited in Jennifer C. Nash, *Black Feminism Reimagined: After Intersectionality* (Durham, NC: Duke University Press, 2019), 116.

2. Nash, *Black Feminism Reimagined*, 116–17.

3. Nash, *Black Feminism Reimagined*, 117.

4. Nash, *Black Feminism Reimagined*, 117.

5. Imani Perry, *Looking for Lorraine: The Radiant and Radical Life of Lorraine Hansberry* (Boston: Beacon, 2018), 162–64.

6. Perry, *Looking for Lorraine*, 163.

7. Perry, *Looking for Lorraine*, 162–64.